Praise for *Catholic Essentials*

"In *Catholic Essentials*, Fr. Wade Menezes, CPM, has taken the cat-echetical content he has imparted and practiced through multiple video series on EWTN and has provided them to the faithful in book form. He preserves his hallmark calm, clarity, and compre-hensiveness, while allowing the reader to readily peruse, study, or pass on the essential doctrines and definitions of our Catholic Faith. He draws constantly from Sacred Scripture, the Fathers and Doctors of the Church, and more recent saints and popes to craft a mosaic—composed of those countless, brilliant, reflective *tesserae* from the Church's treasury—to compose a picture of our faith in Jesus and a reflection of Our Lord, Who is the Way, the Truth, and the Life."

—**Most Reverend Thomas John Paprocki,**
Bishop of Springfield in Illinois

"I highly recommend *Catholic Essentials* for its solid doctrine, moral clarity, and compact practicality. It addresses real questions that ordinary people ask today. It examines real problems that we're all facing. It brings out aspects of the Catholic Faith that the modern world finds vexing and perplexing. And it presents clear answers, explanations, and solutions with admirable brevity."

—**Dr. Scott Hahn, Theology Professor, Franciscan**
University of Steubenville; Founder and President
of the St. Paul Center for Biblical Theology

"As my husband and I made our way back to the Catholic Church some thirty years ago, we were both thrilled and bewildered— thrilled that we were discovering the depth and beauty of Cath-olic teaching for the first time in our lives as cradle Catholics;

bewildered as we wondered how we missed so much for so very long. That's why Fr. Wade's book *Catholic Essentials* is truly an essential resource for Catholics. If your relationship with God, or your understanding of Scripture or doctrine, needs adjusting, look no further than this book. Given the challenges believers are facing from today's toxic culture, *Catholic Essentials* is like a toolbox of truth at your side, helping you implement key elements of the Faith in your everyday life."

—Teresa Tomeo, EWTN Talk-Show Host,
Motivational Speaker, and Best-Selling Author

"This is my third book from Fr. Wade Menezes, and no doubt, it is *essential*. Pun aside, Catholics today really do lack an understanding of the Catholic essentials, from morals and virtues to sacraments and liturgy. This concisely ordered and engagingly written book lays out what we need to know and what we must know to grow in the Faith and in holiness. Fr. Wade continues to make us better Catholics and better people. Get this book for yourself and for your family and friends."

—Paul Kengor, Ph.D., Grove City College,
Author, *The Devil and Karl Marx*

Catholic Essentials

Fr. Wade L. J. Menezes, CPM

Catholic Essentials

A Guide to Understanding
Key Church Teachings

EWTN Publishing, Inc.
Irondale, Alabama

Imprimi Potest: Very Reverend David M. Wilton, CPM,
Superior General, Fathers of Mercy
Nihil Obstat: Colin B. Donovan, S.T.L., *Censor Librorum*
Imprimatur: Most Reverend William F. Medley, D.D.,
Bishop of Owensboro, Kentucky
February 22, 2022, Feast of the Chair of St. Peter

EWTN Publishing, Inc.
5817 Old Leeds Road, Irondale, AL 35210

Distributed by Sophia Institute Press, Box 5284, Manchester, NH 03108.

paperback ISBN 978-1-68278-253-8

ebook ISBN 978-1-68278-254-5

Library of Congress Control Number: 2022931734

3rd printing

For all who practice their Catholic Faith with great fervor,
for the lukewarm,
and for those who have abandoned it: may you soon return.

Contents

Dogma

Ecclesiology

Sacraments

Liturgy

Author's Note

A special note of thanks goes to the United States Conference of Catholic Bishops (Washington, D.C.) for the use of quoted excerpts from the universal *Catechism of the Catholic Church* (CCC), and to Inter Mirifica (Kensington, Maryland) for the use of quoted excerpts from the *Modern Catholic Dictionary* by Fr. John A. Hardon, S.J. As both a baptized Catholic and an ordained Catholic priest, I am indebted to both Pope St. John Paul II and Fr. Hardon for the great clarity with which they taught and continue to teach the Faith to the masses—a clarity that is manifested in a special way because of these two publications.

Introduction

Attain to the unity of the faith and of the knowledge of the Son of God, to mature manhood, to the measure of the stature of the fulness of Christ; so that we may no longer be children, tossed to and fro and carried about with every wind of doctrine, by the cunning of men, by their craftiness in deceitful wiles.

—Ephesians 4:13–14

God is man's glory. Man is the vessel which receives God's action and all his wisdom and power.

—St. Irenaeus[1]

The Catholic Church teaches very clearly that faith is *both* a gift of God *and* a human act. In other words, faith is a great gift that God grants to the individual human person, but it remains up to the individual human person to respond in the affirmative to so great a gift. The *Catechism* bears this all out when it states that faith is "both a *gift of God* and a *human act* by which the believer

---

[1] *Against Heresies*, bk. 3, chap. 20, nos. 2–3: SC 34, 342–344, in *Liturgy of the Hours*, vol. I, 337.

gives personal adherence to God who *invites his response,* and *freely assents to the whole truth that God has revealed.*"[2]

As Catholics, we believe that God has revealed this "whole truth" through Sacred Scripture, Tradition, and the Magisterium— the teaching office of the Church (from the Latin *magister,* which means "teacher"). The *Catechism* continues, "It is this revelation of God which the Church proposes for our belief and which we profess in the *Creed,* celebrate in the *sacraments,* live by *right conduct* that fulfills the twofold commandment of charity (as specified in the Ten Commandments), and respond to in our prayer of faith. Indeed, the *Catechism* sums up, "Faith is both a *theological virtue given by God* as grace, and an *obligation which flows from the first commandment of God.*"[3]

It is clear, then, that such a great gift as faith should be at the very "forefront" of our lives; thus, the need for faithful, clear, and concise catechesis—and the ability to defend it. The purpose of this book is to do just that: provide brief discussions in defense of particular Church teachings. Areas of such teaching include Christology, ecclesiology, the mercy of God, sacraments and sacramentals, the saints, the liturgy, the Eucharist, confession, matrimony, conscience formation, life in society, virtue, sin, the social teaching of the Church, and life and death issues. As faithful Catholics, we should always be ready and willing to lead discussions in defense of the Church's teaching on various matters; indeed, to provide sound catechesis to help others lead better lives directed to "whatever is true, whatever is honorable, whatever is just, whatever is pure, whatever is lovely, whatever is gracious" and "worthy of praise" (see Phil. 4:8).

[2] CCC glossary, s.v. "faith," emphasis added.
[3] CCC glossary, s.v. "faith," emphasis added.

The eighty-one chapters of this book were originally written as catechetical "interstitial" scripts for the Eternal Word Television Network (EWTN). Interstitials are short television spots made to air at the top and bottom of the hour as the day progresses. These chapters come from three distinct interstitial television series I have hosted for EWTN: *Crux of the Matter*, *The Wonders of His Mercy*, and *In Defense of the Eucharist*.

Vatican II teaches us that "every disciple of Christ ... has the duty of spreading the Faith"[4] and that "on all Christians ... is laid the preeminent responsibility of working to make the divine message of salvation known and accepted by all men throughout the world."[5] Amen to both of these teachings. May this book, *Catholic Essentials: A Guide to Understanding Key Church Teachings*, prove to aid us strongly in this regard.

---

[4] Second Vatican Council, Decree on the Mission Activity of the Church *Ad Gentes* (December 2, 1965), no. 23.
[5] Second Vatican Council, Decree on the Apostolate of the Laity *Apostolicam Actuositatem* (November 18, 1965), no. 3.

Morals

Mercy Requires Acknowledging Sin

Have mercy on me, O God,
according to thy steadfast love;
according to thy abundant mercy
blot out my transgressions.
Wash me thoroughly from my iniquity,
and cleanse me from my sin!

—Psalm 51:1-2

We should be displeased with ourselves when we commit sin, for sin is
displeasing to God. Sinful though we are, let us at least be like God in
this, that we are displeased at what displeases him. In some measure
then you will be in harmony with God's will, because you find
displeasing in yourself what is abhorrent to your Creator.

—St. Augustine[6]

In the *Compendium of the Catechism of the Catholic Church*, question 391 asks: "What does the acceptance of God's mercy require from us?" The answer: "It requires that we admit our faults and repent of our sins. God himself, by his word and his Spirit, lays bare our sins

---

[6] *Sermo* 19, 2-3: CCL 41, 252-254, in *Liturgy of the Hours*, vol. III, 451.

and gives us the truth of conscience and the hope of forgiveness." Pope Francis echoes this when he says, "Precisely because there is sin in the world, precisely because our human nature is wounded by original sin, God, who delivered his Son for us, can only reveal himself as merciful. God is a careful and attentive Father, ready to welcome any person who takes a step or even expresses the desire to take a step that leads home."[7]

To receive the great gift of God's mercy requires acknowledging the reality of sin. After all, God's mercy exists precisely because of the reality of sin: the original sin we inherit because of the Fall of our first parents, and any actual, or personal, sin we commit, whether mortal or venial. In other words, if there were no such thing as sin, then there is no need for mercy. But because there is such a thing as sin, there *is* a need for mercy.

Pope Francis has also written, "Mercy exists, but if you don't want to receive it … If you don't recognize yourself as a sinner, it means you don't want to receive it, it means that you don't feel the need for it."[8] All that said, the great news is that no human sin—however serious—can prevail over or limit God's mercy, provided the person seeks repentance of it. In fact, God is so merciful that He can even use one of our sinful falls to draw us more closely to Himself. Maybe this is what Pope Francis means when he states, "I have often said that the place where my encounter with the mercy of Jesus takes place is my sin."[9]

---

[7] Pope Francis, *The Name of God Is Mercy*, trans. Oonagh Stransky (New York: Random House, 2016), 51.
[8] *The Name of God Is Mercy*, 57.
[9] *The Name of God Is Mercy*, 34.

Mercy Calls Us to Be Other-Centered

I will make all my goodness pass before you, and will proclaim before you my name "The Lord"; and I will be gracious to whom I will be gracious, and will show mercy on whom I will show mercy.

—Exodus 33:19

How can a man ask for himself what he refuses to give to another? If he expects to receive any mercy in heaven, he should give mercy on earth. Do we all desire to receive mercy? Let us make mercy our patroness now, and she will free us in the world to come.

—St. Caesarius of Arles[10]

Mercy—often said to be God's greatest attribute—*always* calls us to be "other-centered" as opposed to being "self-centered." Great illustrations of this truth are found in the traditional listing of the so-called Fourteen Works of Mercy, which are geared toward "the other" in an effort precisely to aid them: the seven Corporal Works of Mercy (for the body) and the seven Spiritual Works of Mercy (for the soul) (see "The Fourteen Works of Mercy"). In fact, Fr. John Hardon, S.J., defines mercy as an attribute that deals not only

[10] *Sermo* 25, 1: CCL 103, 111–112, in *Liturgy of the Hours*, vol. III, 547.

with kindness and forgiveness, but also with a "readiness to assist" another. He states that mercy is "the disposition to be kind and forgiving. Founded on compassion, mercy differs from compassion or the feeling of sympathy in putting this feeling into practice with a readiness to assist. It is therefore the ready willingness to help anyone in need, especially in need of pardon or reconciliation."[11] The *Catechism* echoes this when it defines mercy as "the loving kindness, compassion, or forbearance shown to one who offends (e.g., the mercy of God to us sinners)."[12]

Let us not forget the many saints whose lives show us the way of being tirelessly other-centered and merciful. For example, St. Vincent de Paul worked for the poor and disenfranchised; St. Elizabeth Ann Seton educated the young; St. John Bosco aided orphans and helped them develop trades in order to become responsible citizens; and St. Teresa of Calcutta founded the Missionaries of Charity to serve the "poorest of the poor."

Some of my favorite saint quotes about being "other-centered" are the following:

- St. Catherine Labouré (the Miraculous Medal seer) teaches us, "One must see God in everyone."[13]
- St. Peter Chrysologus, an early bishop and Doctor of the Church, says, "If you do not close your ear to others, you open God's ear to yourself."[14]

---

[11] Fr. John A. Hardon, S.J., *Modern Catholic Dictionary* [MCD] (Bardstown, KY: Eternal Life, 1999), 348.

[12] CCC glossary, s.v. "mercy"; see CCC 1422, 1829.

[13] Johnnette Benkovic, *Graceful Living: Meditations to Help You Grow Closer to God Day by Day* (Birmingham, AL: EWTN Publishing, 2016), 339 (cited by Benkovic as "traditionally attributed to St. Catherine Labouré").

[14] From *A Sermon on Prayer, Fasting, and Mercy*; Sermo 43: PL 52, 320, 322, in *Liturgy of the Hours*, vol. II, 231.

• St. Ambrose, the great Doctor of the Church and confessor to St. Augustine, states very eloquently, "No one heals
  himself by wounding another."[15]
• St. Teresa of Calcutta assures us, "Love is a fruit in season
  at all times, and within reach of every hand."[16]

It's been said that the *giving* of oneself brings with it an *enriching* of oneself. What a beautiful thought this is—though it may
sound a little self-centered. Instead, let's really strive to be other-
centered—and especially merciful in forgiveness situations—and
ask the saints of our one, holy, catholic, and apostolic faith to
show us the way.

[15] Ronda Chervin, *Quotable Saints* (Oak Lawn, IL: CMJ Marian
   Publishers, 2003), 68.
[16] *Love: A Fruit Always in Season, Daily Meditations from the Words of
   Mother Teresa of Calcutta*, ed. Dorothy S. Hunt (San Francisco:
   Ignatius Press, 1987), 5.

Mercy toward Others: Some Concrete Actions

So whatever you wish that men would do to you, do so to them; for
this is the law and the prophets.

—Matthew 7:12

Not even night should interrupt you in your duty of mercy. Do not
say: Come back and I will give you something tomorrow.
There should be no delay between your intention and your good deed.
Generosity is the one thing that cannot admit of delay.

—St. Gregory of Nazianzen[17]

As stated previously, mercy is the disposition to be kind and forgiving—a disposition we no doubt want God to practice toward
us. Founded on compassion, mercy is a ready willingness to help
anyone in need, especially those in need of pardon or reconciliation. Now, if we want to receive this great gift from God ourselves,
we also have to be willing to give it to others.

Yet, imitating God in His mercy can seem to be a difficult
task. So, what are some concrete actions—both spiritual and

---

[17] *Oratio* 14, De pauperum amore, 38, 40: PG 35, 907, 910, in *Liturgy*
of the Hours, vol. II, 266.

temporal—that we can sincerely commit to *and* regularly practice to help us become more merciful toward others? I wish to propose just a few such actions, here:

1. Go to the Sacrament of Confession regularly and faithfully—at least once a month—and experience the great gift of God's mercy from this sacrament that our Lord Himself (to St. Faustina) referred to as the "Tribunal of Mercy."[18]

2. Forgive those who have hurt you or done you wrong. Remember the old maxim: "He who angers you, controls you." If you are able and the time is right for both parties, ask for a meeting time with that person to talk and, hopefully, reconcile. This will show sincere effort on your part in being merciful and taking the initiative to help heal the relationship.

3. Read and meditate on the Sacred Scriptures, especially the Gospel of Luke, which is often referred to as the "Gospel of Mercy." St. Luke was a physician. He knows a lot about God's healing and mercy.

4. Be merciful by forgiving debts owed to you and returning collateral whenever possible. Trust in Divine Providence in this regard. Like St. Peter, get out of the boat and walk (see Matt. 14:22–33). But unlike St. Peter at *that* moment, have more faith in Jesus to support you!

5. Pray the Stations of the Cross, weekly if you're able—especially on Fridays at the hour of Divine Mercy: 3:00 p.m.—the very hour in which our Lord died on the

---

[18] See *Diary of St. Maria Faustina Kowalska: Divine Mercy in My Soul* [hereafter *Diary*] (Stockbridge, MA: Marian Press, 1987), nos. 975, 1448.

Cross for us.[19] Thank God for His great mercy shown to all during His "Way of the Cross" and ask Him for the personal grace to become an instrument of His mercy to all.

6. Perform one or more of the corporal and spiritual works of mercy each day (see "The Church's Social Teaching"), and by doing that, share with others (through your kind words and good deeds) the good news of God's mercy manifested in your own life.

7. Pray daily the Divine Mercy Chaplet as our Lord revealed it to St. Faustina, the Divine Mercy seer who revealed it to the world. If you are able, pray it at 3:00 p.m., along with the "Three O'Clock" prayer also taught by our Lord to St. Faustina.[20] If you can't pray these at that time, any time of day will suffice.

8. Donate items to a local pro-life pregnancy center (e.g., diapers, baby food, a stroller, an infant car seat). You'll be helping to defeat the wicked culture of death through a merciful act toward a new mom in need.

9. Pray a novena. Any novena. Commit and consecrate a nine-day period of your life to the Blessed Trinity, the Blessed Virgin Mary, or a saint—any saint. Be bold in your personal petitions and intentions during the novena, praying it first and foremost for the greater glory of God and wanting—in all things—for His will and mercy to be manifested in your life.

10. Live a faith-filled mercy. Get out of your comfort zone and actively involved in your parish. Become a lector,

[19] See *Diary* 1572.
[20] See *Diary* 187, 1319, 1320, 1572.

acolyte, or Extraordinary Minister of Holy Communion at your parish. Become a catechist or church cleaner, or help evangelize the faith door-to-door by making home visitations to both non-Catholics and fallen-away Catholics. There is so much you can commit to at your parish, and every one of these tasks is an opportunity to exhibit the mercy of God toward others.

These are just a few spiritual and temporal suggestions that illustrate how each of us can share the great gift of God's mercy with others. Let us pray that we remain faithful in this important task — and serve as a beacon of God's merciful love in the modern world.

The Fourteen Works of Mercy

And the King will answer them, "Truly, I say to you, as you did it to one of the least of these my brethren, you did it to me."

—Matthew 25:40

The works of mercy are innumerable. Their very variety brings this advantage to those who are true Christians, that in the matter of almsgiving not only the rich and affluent but also those of average means and the poor are able to play their part. Those who are unequal in their capacity to give can be equal in the love within their hearts.

—Pope St. Leo the Great[21]

The fourteen works of mercy hold a special place within the social teaching of the Church: "The *works of mercy* are charitable actions by which we come to the aid of our neighbor in his spiritual and bodily necessities" (CCC 2447). While such actions can surely be many and varied, the Church's traditional listing includes fourteen very important ones: seven for the body (called the "corporal works of mercy" after the Latin word *corpus* which means "body"),

---

[21] *Sermo 6 de Quadragesima*, 1–2: PL 54, 285–287, in *Liturgy of the Hours*, vol. II, 61.

and seven for the soul (called the "spiritual works of mercy"). It is precisely because the human person is a body-soul composite that the fourteen works of mercy are so important in the life of the Christian who is ready and willing to aid his neighbor. So intimate and intricate is the body-soul compositeness of the human person that we can say—and mean it!—that, as human persons, we not only *have* bodies, we *are* bodies; and we not only *have* souls, we *are* souls (see CCC 364–366). So it is, then, that both the *corporal* and *spiritual* realities of the human person need to be attended to and nurtured.

Deeply rooted in Sacred Scripture, the Church's traditional listing of the corporal works of mercy includes: to feed the hungry; to give drink to the thirsty; to clothe the naked; to visit the imprisoned; to shelter the homeless; to visit the sick; and to bury the dead.[22] The spiritual works of mercy are: to admonish the sinner; to instruct the ignorant; to counsel the doubtful; to comfort the sorrowful; to bear wrongs patiently; to forgive all injuries; and to pray for the living and the dead.[23]

Fr. Hardon explains that the corporal works of mercy are the "seven practices of charity, based on Christ's prediction of the Last Judgment (Matt. 5:3–10) that will determine each person's final destiny."[24] He defines the spiritual works of mercy as the "traditional seven forms of Christian charity in favor of the soul or spirit of one's neighbor, in contrast with the corporal works of mercy that minister to people's bodily needs.... Their bases are the teaching of Christ and the practice of the Church since apostolic times."[25]

---

[22] See MCD, 133; CCC 2447.
[23] See MCD, 517.
[24] MCD, 133.
[25] MCD, 517.

One more important point is worth mentioning here: we all know that the liturgical season of Lent encourages increased *prayer, fasting,* and *almsgiving* in one's daily life—what are collectively known as the *three eminent good works.* We can say that the fourteen works of mercy serve as a wonderful blueprint to guide us in our almsgiving *anytime* during the liturgical year, whether as an act of fraternal charity or penitential observance. As Pope St. Gregory the Great says, "When we attend to the needs of those in want, we give them what is theirs, not ours. More than performing works of mercy, we are paying a debt of justice."[26]

---

[26] *Regula Pastoralis.* 3, 21: PL 77, 87, as quoted in CCC 2446.

Importance of a Rightly Formed Conscience

Brethren, I have lived before God in all good conscience up to this day.

—Acts 23:1

Prayer calls us to examine our consciences on all the issues that affect humanity. It calls us to ponder our personal and collective responsibility before the judgment of God and in the light of human solidarity. Hence prayer is able to transform the world.

—St. Pope John Paul II[27]

We live in a day and age when people often—and rightly so—want to make moral decisions based on personal conscience. This is fine and good. But the question remains: is the person making a given decision with a *rightly formed* conscience or with a *wrongly formed* one? Anyone can follow his conscience, but no one should want to make a personal decision based on an erroneous conscience; that is, a conscience that is itself in error. One's conscience ought never be the final arbiter of a decision unless it is, specifically, one that is rightly formed.

According to Church teaching, "Moral conscience, present at the heart of the person, enjoins him at the appropriate moment

---

[27] Address to the bishops of the United States on their Ad Limina visit, June 10, 1988, 4.

to do good and to avoid evil. It also judges particular choices, approving those that are good and denouncing those that are evil" (CCC 1777). Also, "conscience is a judgment of reason whereby the human person recognizes the moral quality of a concrete act that he is going to perform, is in the process of performing, or has already completed" (CCC 1778).

So, how does a person rightly form his conscience? By looking to the teachings of Christ and His Church, upheld by Sacred Scripture, Tradition, and the Magisterium. While the human person "is sometimes confronted with situations that make moral judgments less assured and decisions difficult," one "must always seriously seek what is right and good and discern the will of God expressed in divine law" (CCC 1787).

Church teaching identifies conscience as "the interior voice of a human being, within whose heart the inner law of God is inscribed."[28] Conscience is what moves a person at the appropriate moment to act or to refrain from acting according to that person's understanding of what is good and what is evil. According to Church teaching, "conscience must be informed and moral judgment enlightened. A well-formed conscience is upright and truthful. It formulates its judgments according to reason, in conformity with the true good willed by the wisdom of the Creator" (CCC 1783). So important is the formation of conscience, in fact, that its education "is indispensable for human beings who are subjected to negative influences and tempted by sin to prefer their own judgment and to reject authoritative teachings" (CCC 1783). What a gift human conscience is. Always strive, then, to pursue revealed truth and cooperate with God's grace to help form your conscience correctly and lead it aright.

---

[28] CCC glossary, s.v. "conscience"; see CCC 1454, 1777–1778.

The Seven Gifts of the Holy Spirit

There shall come forth a shoot from the stump of Jesse,
and a branch shall grow out of his roots.
  And the Spirit of the LORD shall rest upon him,
  the spirit of wisdom and understanding,
  the spirit of counsel and might,
  the spirit of knowledge and the fear of the LORD.
And his delight shall be in the fear of the LORD.

−Isaiah 11:1–3

Mary is the stem of the beautiful flower on which the Holy Spirit rests
with the fullness of His gifts. Hence, those who want to obtain the
seven gifts of the Spirit must seek the flower of the Holy Spirit on the
stem [Mary]. We go to Jesus through Mary, and through Jesus we find
the grace of the Holy Spirit.

−St. Bonaventure[29]

The traditional listing of the seven gifts of the Holy Spirit is given
to us in Isaiah 11:1–3: wisdom, understanding, knowledge, counsel,

---

[29] Fr. Frederick Schroeder, *Every Day Is a Gift* (Totowa, NJ: Catholic
Book Publishing, 1984), 123.

piety, fortitude, and fear of the Lord. These gifts are permanent dispositions—habits, in other words—that make a person docile in following the promptings of the Holy Spirit in their daily lived experience.[30] "They belong in their fullness to Christ, Son of David" (CCC 1831), Who is our model for right living and conduct.

These gifts of the Holy Spirit "complete and perfect the virtues of those who receive them. They make the faithful docile in readily obeying divine inspirations" (CCC 1831). They are conferred upon an individual with the reception of sanctifying grace, for example, by making a good, holy and worthily received Sacrament of Confession. The Jesuit theologian Fr. Hardon described the gifts of the Holy Spirit as "seven forms of supernatural initiative" that are "in the nature of supernatural reflexes, or reactive instincts, that spontaneously answer to the divine impulses of grace almost without reflection but always with full consent."[31]

Some theologians posit that these seven gifts are really nothing more than the three theological virtues (faith, hope, and charity) and the four cardinal virtues (prudence, justice, fortitude, and temperance) as exercised in the person's life under the special guidance of the Holy Spirit. But the more common teaching is that they are true, gifted habits that are really distinct from the virtues and which can be practiced in both extraordinary and ordinary circumstances. So, whether during the performance of great heroic acts or during life's more common activities, these seven gifts help us to be prompt and obedient to the divine inspirations of the Holy Spirit.

[30] See CCC glossary, s.v. "gifts of the Holy Spirit"; see CCC 1830.
[31] MCD, 230-231.

The Twelve Fruits of the Holy Spirit

But the fruit of the Spirit is love, joy, peace, patience, kindness, goodness, faithfulness, gentleness, self-control; against such there is no law. And those who belong to Christ Jesus have crucified the flesh with its passions and desires.

—Galatians 5:22-24

Woe to the soul that does not have Christ to cultivate it with care to produce the good fruit of the Holy Spirit. Left to itself, it is choked with thorns and thistles; instead of fruit it produces only what is fit for burning. Woe to the soul that does not have Christ dwelling in it; deserted and foul with the filth of the passions, it becomes a haven for all the vices.

—St. Macarius[32]

Based on Sacred Scripture, the tradition of the Church has identified twelve fruits of the Holy Spirit. These, of course, are tied to our life in Christ Who is our Head and model for right living and conduct. Traditionally, the twelve fruits of the Holy Spirit are listed as: charity, joy, peace, patience, kindness, goodness, generosity, gentleness,

---

[32] Homily attributed to St. Macarius, *Homily* 28: PG 34, 710-711, in *Liturgy of the Hours*, vol. IV, 596.

faithfulness, modesty, self-control, and chastity (see Gal. 5:22–23, Vulgate translation). These twelve fruits are "perfections that the Holy Spirit forms in us as the first fruits of eternal glory" (CCC 1832)—in other words, giving us the earliest glimmerings of the traits and characteristics of eternal life and what it will be like. In theological understanding, a *fruit* is considered to be any virtuous deed in which one delights. This is because they "refresh those that have them, with a holy and genuine delight."[33] The twelve fruits of the Holy Spirit, then, are just that: delights that are products of grace given by the Holy Spirit to a person and that are accompanied by spiritual joy.

These twelve fruits are "supernatural works that, according to St. Paul, manifest the presence of the Holy Spirit. The one who performs them recognizes God's presence by the happiness he experiences, and others the divine presence by witnessing these good works."[34] In other words, those who witness these fruits in someone else behold God's awesome presence working in and through another. So, we may say that these fruits are "identifiable effects of the Holy Spirit"[35] manifesting His power externally in a person's life.

Look at it this way: at first, virtuous acts are often difficult for one to practice on a regular basis—for example, overcoming anger with joy, impatience with patience, or greed with generosity. But when practiced with a certain diligence over time, virtuous acts become easier and easier and are accompanied by a certain spiritual joy—a fruit. It is then that these acts of virtue can be considered fruits in the theological sense—that is, virtuous deeds in which one delights by the prompting and guidance of the Holy Spirit.

[33] *Summa Theologica*, I-II, q. 70, art. 1, quoting St. Ambrose in *De Parad.* xiii.
[34] MCD, 222–223.
[35] MCD, 222–223.

The Three Theological Virtues

So faith, hope, love abide, these three; but the greatest of these is love.

—1 Corinthians 13:13

Faith, hope and love bring safely to God the person who prays, that is, the person who believes, who hopes, who desires, and who ponders what he is asking of the Lord in the Lord's Prayer.

—St. Augustine[36]

When we speak of the three theological virtues of faith, hope, and love (charity), we mean those supernaturally infused good habits that have "the One and Triune God for their origin, motive, and object" (CCC 1812). This makes sense, as the Greek word *Theós* means God, and so anything "*theological*" would pertain to God. Such is the case with these three, specific virtues. In short, then, a theological virtue is a "good habit of the mind or will, supernaturally infused into the soul, whose immediate object is God."[37]

---

[36] *Letter to Proba*, Ep. 130, 12, 22 – 13, 24: CSEL 44, 65-68, in *Liturgy of the Hours*, vol. IV, 422.
[37] MCD, 537.

According to Church teaching, "The human virtues are rooted in the theological virtues, which adapt man's faculties for participation in the divine nature [see 2 Pet. 1:4]: for the theological virtues *relate directly to God*. They dispose Christians to live in a relationship with the Holy Trinity" (CCC 1812, emphasis added).

The source text for the three theological virtues is 1 Corinthians 13:13, wherein St. Paul states, "So faith, hope and love abide, these three; but the greatest of these is love."

According to the *Catechism* (see 1814–1829):

- Faith is the theological virtue by which we believe in God and believe all that he has said and revealed to us, and that Holy Church proposes for our belief, because he is truth itself. By faith, "man freely commits his entire self to God." For this reason the believer seeks to know and do God's will (CCC 1814).

- Hope is the theological virtue by which we desire the kingdom of heaven and eternal life as our happiness, placing our trust in Christ's promises and relying not on our own strength, but on the help of the grace of the Holy Spirit (CCC 1817).

- Charity is the theological virtue by which we love God above all things for his own sake, and our neighbor as ourselves for the love of God (CCC 1822).

The theological virtues are always conferred together with sanctifying grace — for example, when one makes a good, holy, and worthily received Sacrament of Confession. They are the "foundation of Christian moral activity; they animate it and give it its special character. They inform and give life to all the moral virtues" (CCC 1813). Lastly, we can say that these three God-centered theological virtues "are infused by God into the souls of the faithful to make them capable of acting as his children and of meriting eternal life" (CCC 1813). Thus, they are "the pledge of the presence and action of the Holy Spirit in the faculties of the human being" (CCC 1813).

The Four Cardinal Virtues

And if any one loves righteousness, her labors are virtues; for she teaches self-control and prudence, justice and courage; nothing in life is more profitable for men than these.

—Wisdom 8:7

There are, as we know, four cardinal virtues: temperance, justice, prudence, fortitude.

—St. Ambrose[38]

The cardinal virtues (from the Latin word *cardo*, which means *pivot* or *hinge*) are the four *pivotal human virtues*. They are: prudence, justice, fortitude (courage), and temperance (self-control). Look at it this way: If human virtues, in general, are "firm attitudes, stable dispositions, [and] habitual perfections of intellect and will that govern our actions, order our passions, and guide our conduct according to reason and faith" (CCC 1804), then the cardinal virtues are the four primary virtues on which *all other virtues* hinge or pivot. Briefly, the Church teaches the following about the cardinal virtues (see CCC 1805–1809):

---

[38] *Commentary on the Gospel of St. Luke*, bk. V, 62.

- *Prudence* is the virtue that disposes practical reason to discern our true good in every circumstance and to choose the right means of achieving it.... Prudence is "right reason in action," writes St. Thomas Aquinas, following Aristotle [*Summa Theologica*, II-II, Q. 47, art. 2].... it guides the other virtues by setting rule and measure. It is prudence that immediately guides the judgment of conscience. The prudent man determines and directs his conduct in accordance with this judgment. With the help of this virtue we apply moral principles to particular cases without error and overcome doubts about the good to achieve and the evil to avoid. (CCC 1806)
- *Justice* is the moral virtue that consists in the constant and firm will to give their due to God and neighbor. Justice toward God is called the "virtue of religion." Justice toward men disposes one to respect the rights of each and to establish in human relationships the harmony that promotes equity with regard to persons and to the common good. The just man, often mentioned in the Sacred Scriptures, is distinguished by *habitual right thinking* and the *uprightness of his conduct toward his neighbor*. (CCC 1807, emphasis added)
- *Fortitude* is the moral virtue that ensures firmness in difficulties and constancy in the pursuit of the good. It strengthens the resolve to resist temptations and to overcome obstacles in the moral life. The virtue of fortitude enables one to conquer fear, even fear of death, and to face trials and persecutions. It disposes one even to renounce and sacrifice his life in defense of a just cause." (CCC 1808) Fortitude (which is sometimes called courage, strength, or might) is also one of the seven gifts of the Holy Spirit.

• *Temperance* is the moral virtue that moderates the attraction of pleasure and provides balance in the use of created goods. It ensures the will's mastery over instincts and keeps desires within the limits of what is honorable. The temperate person directs the sensitive appetites toward what is good and maintains a healthy discretion. (CCC 1809)

Holy Mother Church obtains her teaching on the four cardinal virtues from the Book of Wisdom 8:7, wherein we read: "And if any one loves righteousness, her labors are virtues; for she teaches self-control and prudence, justice and courage; nothing in life is more profitable for men than these." So, then, let our daily lives "hinge" on these four wonderful cardinal virtues.

The Three Eminent Good Works

And when Jesus saw that a crowd came running together, he rebuked the unclean spirit, saying to it, "You dumb and deaf spirit, I command you, come out of him, and never enter him again." And after crying out and convulsing him terribly, it came out, and the boy was like a corpse; so that most of them said, "He is dead." But Jesus took him by the hand and lifted him up, and he arose. And when he had entered the house, his disciples asked him privately, "Why could we not cast it out?" And he said to them, "This kind cannot be driven out by anything but prayer and fasting."

—Mark 9:25–29

To your praying add fasting and almsgiving. It is on these wings that our prayers fly the more swiftly and effortlessly to the holy ears of God, that He may mercifully hear us in the time of need.

—Pope Innocent III[39]

The *Catechism* teaches that "the interior penance of the Christian can be expressed in many and various ways. Scripture and the

[39] Quoted by Pope St. John XXIII, Encyclical *Paenitentiam Agere* (July 1, 1962), no. 19.

Fathers insist above all on three forms, *fasting, prayer,* and *almsgiving*" (CCC 1434). Indeed, the "three principal good works in Christianity are prayer, fasting, and almsgiving."[40] These three spiritual actions, practiced within a sound and dedicated spiritual life, are referred to as the three "eminent good works"[41] in the life of the Church. They are important because they help "express conversion in relation to oneself, to God, and to others" (CCC 1434) — again, via a disposition of interior penance. Let's take a brief look at each:

- Prayer is "the elevation of the mind and heart to God in praise of His glory; a petition made to God for some desired good, or in thanksgiving for a good received, or in intercession for others before God. Through prayer the Christian experiences a communion with God through Christ in the Church."[42] Prayer is the "voluntary response to the awareness of God's presence. This response may be an acknowledgment of God's greatness and of a person's total dependence on him (adoration), or gratitude for his benefits to oneself and others (thanksgiving), or sorrow for sins committed and begging for mercy (expiation), or asking for graces needed (petition), or affection for God, who is all good (love)."[43]
- Fasting entails "refraining from food and drink as an expression of interior penance, in imitation of the fast of Jesus for forty days in the desert. Fasting is an ascetical practice recommended in Scripture and the writings of the Church Fathers; it is sometimes prescribed by a precept

---

[40] MCD, 182.
[41] MCD, 182.
[42] CCC glossary, s.v. "prayer"; see CCC 1434, 2559–2565.
[43] MCD, 431.

of the Church, especially during the liturgical season of Lent."[44] Fasting can be said to be "a form of penance that imposes limits on the kind or quantity of food or drink"[45] one may take. But fasting can also include refraining from and limiting the use of non-food products like television, the Internet, shopping, sports, and the like.

• And lastly, almsgiving consists of the "money or goods given to the poor as an act of penance or fraternal charity. Almsgiving, together with prayer and fasting, are traditionally recommended to foster the state of interior penance."[46] In short, the giving of alms refers to the "material or financial assistance given to a needy person or cause, prompted by Christian charity. Almsgiving is recognized by the Church as one of the principal forms of penance, especially since the mitigation of laws on fast and abstinence"[47] since the Second Vatican Council (Vatican II).

What a gift the "three eminent good works" are! They aid not only those who practice them, but also those who may benefit from efforts on their behalf (e.g., praying for others, fasting for others). So, let us practice these eminent good works not only during the liturgical season of Lent, but throughout the entire liturgical year, making them a prominent part of the spiritual life.

[44] CCC glossary, s.v. "fasting"; see CCC 538, 1434, 2043.
[45] MCD, 207.
[46] CCC glossary, s.v. "almsgiving"; see CCC 1434, 1969, 2447.
[47] MCD, 19.

Devotion

*Do bear with me! I feel a divine jealousy for you, for I betrothed you
to Christ to present you as a pure bride to her one husband. But I am
afraid that as the serpent deceived Eve by his cunning, your thoughts
will be led astray from a sincere and pure devotion to Christ.*

—2 Corinthians 11:1–3

*I say that devotion must be practiced in different ways by the
nobleman and by the working man, by the servant and by the prince,
by the widow, by the unmarried girl and by the married woman. But
even this distinction is not sufficient; for the practice of devotion must
be adapted to the strength, to the occupation and to the duties of each
one in particular.*

—St. Francis de Sales[48]

As Catholics, we're keen on devotion and acts of devotion. Whether
it be attending holy Mass faithfully, partaking of the Sacrament
of Penance regularly, praying the Rosary or the Chaplet of Divine
Mercy daily, attending a novena, using holy water in and outside

---

[48] *Introduction to the Devout Life*, Pars 1, cap. 3, in *Liturgy of the Hours*,
vol. III, 1318.

the home, or having a devotion to a certain patron saint by wearing a religious medal that depicts him or her, we acknowledge these sacraments and sacramentals as part of our Catholic devotional life. But what, exactly, is "devotion" according to the teaching tradition of the Church?

Devotion is the "disposition of will to do promptly what concerns the worship and service of God. Although devotion is primarily a disposition or attitude of the will, acts of the will that proceed from such disposition are also expressions of devotion."[49] An essential and key component to devotion is "readiness to do whatever gives honor to God, whether in public or private prayer (worship) or in doing the will of God (service). A person who is thus disposed is said to be devoted. His devotedness is ultimately rooted in a great love for God, which in spiritual theology is often called devotion."[50] And let's not forget: Ideally, with one's great love for God, one inevitably moves toward a great love for neighbor, as well.

So it is that devotion can be said to feed and inspire not only one's spiritual life (through prayer and worship), but also one's temporal (or secular) life (through acts of service). I've met many Catholics, for example, who not only exude their Christianity simply and devotedly while engaged in prayer and worship, but also do so while carrying out their everyday activities within their family and work environments. I take notice, too, that this takes place regardless of a person's vocation and state in life—whether single, married, widowed, or a consecrated Religious, deacon, priest, or bishop.

[49] MCD, 156.
[50] MCD, 156.

Therefore, we can say that authentic devotion—while primarily a disposition or attitude of the will to do promptly what concerns the worship and service of God—actually moves one to a greater love of *both* God *and* neighbor. What a gift this is to God, to others, and to self!

The Importance of Making a Spiritual Retreat

And he said to them, "Come away by yourselves to a lonely place, and rest a while."

—Mark 6:31

Days on retreat. Recollection in order to know God, to know yourself and thus to make progress. A necessary time for discovering where and how you should change your life. What should I do? What should I avoid?

—St. Josemaría Escrivá[51]

Widely neglected in our day and age, but of great importance for growth in the spiritual life and for the ordering of one's temporal life, is the occasional making of a spiritual retreat—at least annually. This is true for everyone, regardless of their vocation and state in life. As noted by Pope Benedict XVI (writing as Joseph Cardinal Ratzinger), "Without doubt, a Christian needs certain periods of retreat into solitude to be recollected and, in God's presence,

---

[51] St. Josemaría Escrivá, *Furrow*, no. 177, Josemaría Escrivá, https://www.escrivaworks.org/book/furrow.htm.

rediscover his path."[52] A time of spiritual retreat refreshes the whole person—soul, body, mind, and spirit. It provides time for contemplation and prayer—in short, it's a time for "friendly intercourse, and frequent solitary converse, with him who we know loves us."[53]

The word *retreat* means to "pull away from" or to "pull back" and is associated with military combat—for example, when soldiers in combat pull away from or retreat from the front line of battle. When making a good retreat, that's exactly what the Christian is doing: he or she is pulling back from the affairs of everyday life and reconnecting with God in a special way in surroundings that are conducive to this end. A retreat involves a "withdrawal for a period of time from one's usual surroundings and occupations to a place of solitude for meditation, self-examination, and prayer, in order to make certain necessary decisions in one's spiritual life. Although the practice is older than Christianity, the example of Christ's forty days in the desert makes such retreats part of divine revelation, to be imitated, as far as possible, by his followers."[54]

According to Fr. Hardon, who was a renowned retreat master himself, "As a formal devotion among all classes of the faithful, retreats were introduced with the Counter-Reformation, led by St. Ignatius of Loyola, and followed by St. Francis de Sales and St. Vincent de Paul."[55] In reference to the Church's Canon Law, Fr. Hardon also notes that "retreats for a specified number of days are required annually of all priests and religious."[56]

---

[52] Congregation for the Doctrine of the Faith, *Letter to the Bishops of the Catholic Church on Some Aspects of Christian Meditation* (October 15, 1989).

[53] St. Teresa of Avila, *Life*, chap. 8.

[54] MCD, 466.

[55] MCD, 466.

[56] MCD, 466.

Worth noting, too, is that Pope Pius XI, in his *Apostolic Constitution Declaring St. Ignatius Patron of all Spiritual Exercises* (July 25, 1922), wrote: "We desire that retreat houses, where persons withdraw for a month, or for eight days, or for fewer, to put themselves into training for the perfect Christian life, may come into being and flourish everywhere more numerously." So it is that many Religious orders own, staff, and operate retreat houses or retreat centers, as do some dioceses and Catholic lay-based organizations. All of these will offer calendars of specifically themed retreats (e.g., for individuals, married couples, fathers and sons, mothers and daughters, Ignatian, etc.) and will also give the name and credentials of the retreat master giving the retreat.

One final note: While a registration fee is often required for a spiritual retreat, it is usually a reasonable one, given the costs associated with hosting a group of persons at a retreat center (such as food, utilities, groundskeeping, and general staffing). So, do some research and check out what Catholic retreat houses exist in your diocese and surrounding area. Make sure they're reputable for their faithfulness to the teaching of the Church, and then invest in your spiritual life—and make a spiritual retreat.

The Seven Capital Sins and Their Opposite Corresponding Virtues

You have heard that it was said, "You shall not commit adultery." But I say to you that every one who looks at a woman lustfully has already committed adultery with her in his heart.

—Matthew 5:27–28

A man who governs his passions is master of the world. We must either command them, or be enslaved by them. It is better to be a hammer than an anvil.

—St. Dominic[57]

A well-versed Christian should always be prepared to articulate the theological teaching behind the seven capital sins (or vices), so as to protect himself and others, knowing the harm they can do to the human person. What makes a sin capital? The *Catechism* identifies as the seven capital sins those that "engender other sins, other vices. They are pride, avarice, envy, wrath, lust, gluttony, and sloth or acedia" (CCC 1866).

---

[57] Chervin, *Quotable Saints*, 68.

The great Doctor of the Church, St. Francis de Sales, in his famous work, *Introduction to the Devout Life*, says, "When we are assailed by some vice, we must, as far as possible, embrace the practice of the contrary virtue."[58] This is sound advice, indeed: to literally *practice* the opposite virtues—with one's sensory and spiritual powers—in concrete *daily* actions (see CCC 1803) in order to overcome the very vice that one is attached to.

All of this reflects the truth that each of the seven capital sins—as a *vice*—has an opposite, corresponding *virtue*. This is simply another way of saying that "vices can be classified according to the virtues they oppose" (CCC 1866). So, let's comb through the Church's traditional list of seven capital sins and contrast them with their opposite virtues: for pride, the corresponding virtue is humility; for avarice (or greed), it's generosity; for envy, brotherly love; for wrath (or anger), meekness; for lust, chastity; for gluttony, temperance; for sloth (or acedia), it's diligence. Note: We can rightly call these seven opposite corresponding virtues the "capital virtues," precisely because they are the counterparts to the seven "capital vices."

While every Christian should surely be able to name and identify the capital sins, let us not forget that in a sound, moral life, we should be just as eager to name and identify their opposite, corresponding virtues. Living a strong, dedicated moral life demands this catechetical balance.

---

[58] St. Francis de Sales, *Introduction to the Devout Life* (Wheathampstead, Hertfordshire: Anthony Clark Books, 1962), pt. III, chap. 1.

Mortal Sin and Venial Sin

*If any one sees his brother committing what is not a mortal sin, he
will ask, and God will give him life for those whose sin is not mortal.
There is sin which is mortal; I do not say that one is to pray for that.
All wrongdoing is sin, but there is sin which is not mortal.*

—1 John 5:16–17

*Two things alone I fear: mortal sin which kills the soul, and dying
in mortal sin. I fear that some of you may fall victims of your own
negligence of your spiritual welfare. Death skips no one.*

—St. John Bosco[59]

According to the teaching tradition of the Church, "Sins are rightly
evaluated according to their gravity" (CCC 1854). Catholic teaching
acknowledges two distinctions or categories of sin, which indicate
this gravity: "mortal" and "venial."

Mortal sin is a grave violation of the law of God that destroys the divine life in the soul of the sinner; that is, it destroys

---

[59] From a November 1858 talk that he gave to a group of boys, as
quoted in Rev. Giovanni Battista Lemoyne, S.D.B., *The Biographical
Memoirs of Saint John Bosco*, trans. Rev. Diego Borgatello, S.D.B.
(New Rochelle: Salesiana Publishers, 1971), 40.

sanctifying grace in the soul that makes one an actual participator in the divine life of God. The *Catechism*, quoting Pope St. John Paul II's landmark Post-Synodal Apostolic Exhortation, *Reconciliation and Penance* (*Reconciliatio et Paenitentia*, December 2, 1984), teaches that three elements must together be present for a mortal sin to have been committed: "For a *sin* to be *mortal*, three conditions must together be met: 'Mortal sin is sin whose object is grave matter and which is also committed with full knowledge and deliberate consent' "[60] (CCC 1857). So it is, then, that "*mortal sin* destroys charity in the heart of man by a grave violation of God's law; it turns man away from God, who is his ultimate end and his beatitude, by preferring an inferior good to him" (CCC 1855). The truth should not be taken lightly, then, that "mortal sin is a radical possibility of human freedom.... It results in the loss of charity and the privation of sanctifying grace, that is, of the state of grace. If it is not redeemed by repentance and God's forgiveness, it causes exclusion from Christ's kingdom and the eternal death of hell, for our freedom has the power to make choices for ever, with no turning back" (CCC 1861).

As regards venial sin, the Church teaches that, "One commits *venial sin* when, in a less serious matter, he does not observe the standard prescribed by the moral law, or when he disobeys the moral law in a grave matter, but *without* full knowledge or *without* complete consent" (CCC 1862, emphasis added). Furthermore, "Venial sin weakens charity; it manifests a disordered affection for created goods; it impedes the soul's progress in the exercise of the virtues and the practice of the moral good" (CCC 1863). And while "venial sin does not deprive the sinner of sanctifying

---

[60] Pope St. John Paul II, Post-synodal Apostolic Exhortation *Reconciliatio et Paenitentia* (December 2, 1984), no. 17§12.

grace, friendship with God, charity, and consequently eternal happiness,"[61] we must not forget that, "deliberate and unrepented venial sin disposes us little by little to commit mortal sin" (CCC 1863). So, for any transgression of the law, if any one of the three requirements for a mortal sin is absent, then a venial sin is present. Remember: Venial sin still allows sanctifying grace—that is, divine life—to subsist in the soul, but it weakens it; and while venial sin does not destroy charity in the human heart, it does offend and wound it (see CCC 1855).

The *Catechism* teaches, "The distinction between mortal sin and venial sin, already evident in Scripture, became part of the tradition of the Church. It is corroborated by human experience" (CCC 1854). In 1 John 5:16-17, for example, we learn that while all sin is wrongdoing, there is sin that is mortal and sin that is not mortal. And whereas mortal sin merits eternal punishment in Hell, venial sin merits temporal punishment either on earth or in Purgatory. Once a mortal sin is forgiven in the Sacrament of Confession, however, it then merits temporal punishment. Venial sin, while it can surely be confessed in the Sacrament of Penance, can also be forgiven by making an act of *perfect* contrition. An act of *perfect* contrition is worded in such a way that it makes clear that one is *primarily* sorry for their sins precisely because they have offended God and *secondarily* because those same sins threaten one with punishment by one's own wrongdoing that was freely-chosen. So-called *imperfect* contrition is the opposite of this. Let us strive—sincerely—to shun all sin, whether mortal *or* venial.

---

[61] *Reconciliatio et Paenitentia*, 17§9.

Sins Against the Holy Spirit

*Therefore I tell you, every sin and blasphemy will be forgiven men, but
the blasphemy against the Spirit will not be forgiven. And whoever says
a word against the Son of man will be forgiven; but whoever speaks
against the Holy Spirit will not be forgiven, either in this age or in the
age to come.*

—Matthew 12:31–32

You must keep your soul innocent and free from deceit.

*The present is a time for the acknowledgment of sins. Acknowledge
what you have done, in word or deed, by night or day. Acknowledge
your sins at a time of God's favor, and on the day of salvation you will
receive the treasures of heaven.*

*Wash yourself clean, so that you may hold a richer store of grace.
Sins are forgiven equally for all, but communion in the Holy Spirit is
given in the measure of each one's faith.*

—St. Cyril of Jerusalem[62]

Sins against the Holy Spirit are "major offenses that carry a stubborn
resistance to the inspirations of the Holy Spirit and a contempt of

---

[62] *Cat.* 1, 2–3. 5–6: PG 33, 371, 375–378, in *Liturgy of the Hours*, vol.
III, 445–446.

His gifts."[63] In short, they are mortal sins (in that they constitute grave matter) that harden a soul by its rejection of the Holy Spirit and His ability *to work in, through, and transform* that soul.

The teaching tradition of the Church lists six such sins. They are: presumption of God's mercy and forgiveness; despair of God's mercy concerning the possibility of one's salvation; opposing, resisting, or attacking known truths of the Faith; envy of another's spiritual good and growth; obstinacy and persistence in sin; and final impenitence and refusal to turn to God before death.

Sins against the Holy Spirit are most grave and serious because they reject the Third Person of the Holy Trinity Who was sent by the Father to sanctify us and restore us to full communion with Him. While sins can be committed against one's neighbor, sins against the Holy Spirit are immediately and directly against God Himself. They challenge and undermine the Christian life, for neither *faith, hope,* nor *charity* (the three theological virtues) are possible when God is directly and immediately rejected through such sins. This is why these sins against the Holy Spirit are sometimes also referred to as "sins against the theological virtues."

In the Gospel, our Lord mentions the "sin against the Holy Spirit" as the so-called "unforgivable sin" (see Matt. 12:31–32). The Church's teaching tradition holds that these sins against the Holy Spirit are called such precisely because those "who sin in this way, resisting grace, do not wish to repent"[64] and so it is said that "their sins cannot be forgiven them."[65] For example, with the sin of final impenitence and refusal to turn to God before death, one *willingly* and *knowingly* rejects God and His grace from working

---

[63] MCD, 507.
[64] MCD, 508.
[65] MCD, 508.

in his life while near death. This final impenitence is most often caused by either despair or presumption of God's mercy. At the same time, however, the "unforgivable sin" against the Holy Spirit is really *any* purposefully unrepentant mortal sin that one refuses to turn over to God for forgiveness—whether near death or not. And let's note: It's unforgivable *not* because of our Lord or His Bride, the Church—after all, it's the Church who sent the priest to the person's bedside to administer the Last Rites! Rather, it's unforgivable because of his own stubborn resistance to the grace of the Holy Spirit. Remember: *Any* sin can be forgiven, provided the person willfully seeks forgiveness. This is why sorrow for one's sins and repentance of them is so important—especially for mortal sins.

Sins That Cry to Heaven

Beloved, never avenge yourselves, but leave it to the wrath of God; for it is written, "Vengeance is mine, I will repay, says the Lord."

—Romans 12:19

Do not despair of his [God's] mercy, no matter how great your sins, for great mercy will take away great sins.

For the Lord is gracious and merciful and prefers the conversion of a sinner rather than his death. Patient and generous in his mercy, he does not give in to human impatience but is willing to wait a long time for our repentance. So extraordinary is the Lord's mercy in the face of evil, that if we do penance for our sins, he regrets his own threat and does not carry out against us the sanctions he had threatened.

—St. Jerome[66]

As with the previous chapter, "Sins Against the Holy Spirit," this chapter, too, involves the reality of grave matter that constitutes mortal sin. And when done with fullness of knowledge and deliberate consent, its result is to deny a soul entrance into Heaven (see

---

[66] From a commentary on the book of Joel, PL 25, 967–968, in *Liturgy of the Hours*, vol. IV, 178.

"Mortal and Venial Sin"). It's worth recalling, here, that mortal sin deprives a soul of God's sanctifying grace because it is a serious transgression of God's law. Such are the "Sins That Cry to Heaven."

The Church's traditional listing of the sins that cry to Heaven include willful murder (see Gen. 4:10); sodomy and homosexual activity (see Gen. 18:20–21); oppression of the poor, including widows and orphans (see Exod. 2:23); and defrauding laborers of their just wages (see James 5:4).[67] Passages from Sacred Scripture tell of the gravity of these sins, and both Sacred Tradition and the Church's constant magisterial teaching confirm their grave sinfulness. These sins are said to cry to Heaven precisely because they militate directly against the dignity of the human person—in a way contrary to the image and likeness of God in which the human person is made (see Gen. 1:26-27).

A definition that applies to the three divine Persons of the Holy Trinity is that They are "a community of Persons living in communion." Interestingly, the same definition can be applied to all of humanity! That is, all of us, too, are "a community of persons living in communion." And we are all made in the image and likeness of God as taught in the Book of Genesis. By their very nature, then, the sins that cry to Heaven disrupt the communion we are called to with our Triune God *and* with each other.

Willful murder; sins against human nature and the natural law that deny the proper purpose and use of the human body; oppression of the poor, widows, and orphans; and defrauding laborers of their just wages are serious offenses against the human person. Everyone has a right to life—even the baby in utero. Every person should see his body as a true temple of the Holy Spirit that is home to a human soul capable of receiving God's sanctifying

[67] See MCD, s.v. "Sins Crying to Heaven," 508.

grace and becoming a partaker in the divine nature, thereby actually participating in God's own divine life (see 2 Pet. 1:4). The poor, widows, and orphans should never suffer oppression, but should be cared for. And laborers deserve a just wage. As the *Catechism* teaches, "A *just wage* is the legitimate fruit of work. To refuse or withhold it can be a grave injustice" (CCC 2434).

Let us remember that *any* sin—regardless of how serious or grave it might be—can always be forgiven, provided the person is sincerely contrite and asks for forgiveness from God, the loving Father of mercies, through His Son, in the Holy Spirit. And let us remember also the important Christian maxim to *always love the sinner, but hate the sin.*

Four Consequences of Personal Sin

And to Adam he said, "Because you have listened to the voice of your wife, and have eaten of the tree of which I commanded you, 'You shall not eat of it,' cursed is the ground because of you; in toil you shall eat of it all the days of your life; thorns and thistles it shall bring forth to you; and you shall eat the plants of the field. In the sweat of your face you shall eat bread till you return to the ground, for out of it you were taken; you are dust, and to dust you shall return."

—Genesis 3:17–19

Whoever is in Christ is a new creation; the old has passed away. *Now, by the "new creation" Paul means the indwelling of the Holy Spirit in a heart that is pure and blameless, free of all malice, wickedness or shamefulness. For when a soul has come to hate sin and has delivered itself as far as it can to the power of virtue, it undergoes a transformation by receiving the grace of the Spirit. Then it is healed, restored and made wholly new. Indeed the two texts:* Purge out the old leaven that you may be a new one, *and:* Let us celebrate the festival, not with the old leaven but with the unleavened bread of sincerity and truth, *support those passages which speak about the new creation.*

—St. Gregory of Nyssa[68]

---

[68] From a book on Christian formation, PG 46, 295–298, in *Liturgy of the Hours*, vol. IV, 337–338.

As Christians, we know that sin is always a personal act. That is, even though a particular sin might be carried out in concert with another (as in the case of adultery) or with others, sin is always committed according to one's personal choice. Also, the time-honored teaching of the Church has always defined sin not only as an offense against one's reason and right conscience, but also against God and against truth (see CCC 1849–1850).

Understanding that our sin always offends in an ever-widening sphere (from the individual to the Eternal), the Church teaches that there are four categorical consequences to every sin: *personal, social, ecclesial,* and *cosmic.* In other words, each and every sin committed—whether venial or mortal—somehow and in some way affects the individual *personally* (say, by friction with self—for example, constriction in the growth of virtue); *socially* (by wounding his relationship with others); *ecclesially* (by disrupting the body of Christ, the Church); and *cosmically* (just read Gen. 3 or Rom. 8:20–21 to see how the very cosmos—creation itself—was affected by the Fall of our first parents, which ushered in Original Sin).

The good news, however, is that these four areas of disruption are healed through the Sacrament of Reconciliation (Confession) because of the sinner's seeking of forgiveness and Almighty God's mercy and divine intervention. In fact, "it must be emphasized that *the most precious result* of the forgiveness obtained in the Sacrament of Penance consists in *reconciliation with God,* which takes place in the inmost heart of the son who was lost and found again, which every penitent is."[69] But there's more. Regarding the four areas of disruption, the *Catechism,* quoting our late Holy Father, Pope St. John Paul II, states, "It must be recalled that ... this reconciliation with God leads, as it were, to *other reconciliations,* which repair the

---

[69] *Reconciliatio et Paenitentia* 31§5, emphasis added; see Luke 15:17–21.

other breaches caused by sin. The forgiven penitent is reconciled with *himself* in his inmost being, where he regains his innermost truth. He is reconciled with his *brethren* whom he has in some way offended and wounded. He is reconciled with the *Church*. He is reconciled with all *creation*"[70] (CCC 1469).

So, just as there is disruption between the sinner and these four areas, there is also healing between the penitent and these four areas. This is indeed the good news of reconciliation—the good news of salvation.

---

[70] *Reconciliatio et Paenitentia* 31§5.

On Giving Scandal to Others

So put away all malice and all guile and insincerity and envy and all slander. Like newborn babes, long for the pure spiritual milk, that by it you may grow up to salvation; for you have tasted the kindness of the Lord.

—1 Peter 2:1–3

We should even go beyond doing what is required in order to avoid scandal.

—St. Basil the Great[71]

Church teaching defines scandal as "an attitude or behavior which leads another to do evil" (CCC 2284). The *Catechism* states, "The person who gives scandal becomes his neighbor's tempter. He damages virtue and integrity; he may even draw his brother into spiritual death. Scandal is a grave offense if by deed or omission another is deliberately led into a grave offense" (CCC 2284).

It is interesting to note that the *Catechism* talks about scandal under the heading of "Respect for the Dignity of Persons." This

---

[71] Paul Thigpen, *A Dictionary of Quotes from the Saints* (Ann Arbor, MI: Servant Publications, 2001), 200.

makes sense, as the very dignity of human persons requires that evil, in all forms, be avoided. "Scandal takes on a particular gravity by reason of the authority of those who cause it or the weakness of those who are scandalized.... Scandal is grave when given by those who by nature or office are obliged to teach and educate others. Jesus reproaches the scribes and Pharisees on this account: he likens them to wolves in sheep's clothing" (CCC 2285; see Matt. 7:15).

Echoing the teaching Tradition of the Church, Fr. Hardon makes a distinction between *direct* and *indirect* scandal: "Direct scandal, also called diabolical, has the deliberate intention to induce another to sin. In indirect scandal a person does something that he or she foresees will at least likely lead another to commit sin, but this is rather tolerated than positively desired."[72] Still, scandal is "any action or its omission, not necessarily sinful in itself [although it well may be], that is likely to induce another to do something morally wrong."[73]

It must be noted, too, that scandal is provoked not only by individuals, but also "by laws or institutions, by fashion or opinion" (CCC 2286). Pope Pius XII once stated, "They are guilty of scandal who establish laws or social structures leading to the decline of morals and the corruption of religious practice, or to 'social conditions that, intentionally or not, make Christian conduct and obedience to the Commandments difficult and practically impossible.' "[74]

To summarize, then, manipulators of public opinion who turn it away from moral values, or "anyone who uses the power at his disposal in such a way that it leads others to do wrong becomes

[72] MCD, 491.
[73] MCD, 491.
[74] Radio message for Pentecost 1941 (June 1, 1941), quoted in CCC 2286.

guilty of scandal and responsible for the evil that he has *directly* or *indirectly* encouraged" (CCC 2287; emphasis added). As our Lord states in the Gospel, "Temptations to sin are sure to come, but woe to him by whom they come!" (Luke 17:1).

On Being an Accessory to Sin

Whoever causes one of these little ones who believe in me to sin, it would be better for him if a great millstone were hung round his neck and he were thrown into the sea.

—Mark 9:42

For the sake of eternal life, my brothers, let us do the will of the Father who called us, resisting the temptations that lead us into sin and striving earnestly to advance in virtue. Let us revere God for fear of the evils that spring from impiety.

—From a *homily written in the second century*[75]

Related to the Church's teaching on scandal is the additional teaching that one can act as an "accessory" to another's sin. As faithful Christians, we not only want to keep ourselves away from sin, but we want to help keep others away from it. We know well from our catechesis that sin is an offense against God as well as against reason, truth, and right conscience. It is defined by St. Augustine as "an utterance, a deed, or a desire contrary to the

---

[75] Cap. 10, 1-12, 1; 13, 1: Funk 1, 157-159, in *Liturgy of the Hours*, vol. IV, 516.

eternal law"[76] (CCC 1849). We must seek to avoid sin and sinful behavior at all costs.

This seems obvious enough in regard to one's carrying out a sinful action individually; but what about a person serving as an "accessory" to another's sin? By accessory, here, I am referring to one's *aiding* or *abetting* another in their sin. According to the Church's moral Tradition, there are nine ways of being an accessory to another's sin. Rev. F. X. Lasance and Rev. Francis Augustine Walsh, O.S.B., in *The New Roman Missal*, provide us with the list: "1. By counsel. 2. By command. 3. By consent. 4. By provocation. 5. By praise or flattery. 6. By concealment. 7. By partaking. 8. By silence. 9. By defense of the ill [sinful action] done."[77] These are all ways in which a person can aid or abet another in his sin. An example of this is the person who drives a woman to an abortion clinic to have an abortion. The driver, by the very act of driving the woman to the clinic for that purpose, partakes in, provokes, and defends this sinful action. One could also argue that by doing so, the driver is—at least indirectly—giving both counsel and consent to the abortion, as well.

The *Catechism* also outlines this concept of "cooperation" in the sin of others:

> Sin is a personal act. Moreover, we have a responsibility for the sins committed by others *when we cooperate in them*:
>
> • by participating directly and voluntarily in them;
> • by ordering, advising, praising, or approving them;

---

[76] St. Augustine, *Contra Faustum* 22: *PL* 42, 418; St. Thomas Aquinas, *Summa Theologica*, I-II, q. 71, art. 6.

[77] Rev. F. X. Lasance and Rev. Francis Augustine Walsh, O.S.B., *The New Roman Missal* (New York: Benziger Brothers, 1942), 1795.

• by not disclosing or not hindering them when we have an obligation to do so;

• by protecting evil-doers.

Thus sin makes men accomplices of one another and causes concupiscence, violence, and injustice to reign among them. Sins give rise to social situations and institutions that are contrary to the divine goodness. "Structures of sin" are the expression and effect of personal sins. They lead their victims to do evil in their turn. In an analogous sense, they constitute a "social sin" (CCC 1868-1869).

Sin is no matter to be taken lightly. It is always dangerous, harmful, and hurtful to self and others. By its very nature, "it is failure in genuine love for God and neighbor.... It wounds the nature of man and injures human solidarity" (CCC 1849). While we surely want to stay away from committing any sin individually and personally, we likewise never want to be an accessory to another's sin—for that, too, is sinful behavior if done willfully.

Theology of the Body

May the God of peace himself sanctify you wholly; and may your
spirit and soul and body be kept sound and blameless at the coming of
our Lord Jesus Christ

– 1 Thessalonians 5:23

The human body, oriented interiorly by the sincere gift of the person,
reveals not only its masculinity or femininity on the physical plane, but
reveals also such a value and such a beauty as to go beyond the purely
physical dimension of sexuality.

– Pope St. John Paul II[78]

The Church receives her teachings on the "theology" of the human body from several important sources—first of all, from her rich, pedagogical patrimony on the dignity of the human person made in the image and likeness of God (see Gen. 1:26-27) and as the only creature God has willed for its own sake.[79] The teachings of Pope St. John

---

[78] Wednesday Audience, January 16, 1980.
[79] See Second Vatican Council, Pastoral Constitution on the Church in the Modern World *Gaudium et Spes* (December 7, 1965), no. 24 3; CCC 356, 1703.

Paul II also contribute greatly to this area of study, most notably his 129 papal audiences devoted to the subject and given at the Vatican from September 1979 through November 1984. But there's more: natural law, revealed moral law, science, and ontology—that branch of metaphysics dealing with the nature of being—all contribute in their own important ways to the study of the "theology of the body."

But what, exactly, does "theology of the body" mean? In breaking down the phrase, we know that "theology" is the study of God (from the Greek *theos*, "god" and *logia* [*logy*], "study of"); we know, too, that when we say "body" here, we mean it specifically in reference to the *human* body. Thus, the phrase "theology of the body" could be defined as "the study of God *in*, *through*, and *about* the *meaning*, *reality*, and *being* of the human body." The *magnus corpus* of Pope St. John Paul II on this topic, especially, provides a most succinct manner in which to approach it and study it.

> The "Theology of the Body" is St. John Paul II's integrated vision of the human person. The human body has a specific meaning, making visible an invisible reality, and is capable of revealing answers regarding fundamental questions about us and our lives:
> - Is there a real purpose to life, and if so, what is it?
> - What does it mean that we were created in the image of God?
> - Why were we created male and female? Does it really matter if we are one sex or the other?
> - What does the marital union of a man and a woman say to us about God and His plan for our lives?
> - What is the purpose of the married and celibate vocations?
> - What exactly is love?

• Is it truly possible to be pure of heart?

All of these questions, and many more, are answered in the 129 Wednesday audiences popularly known as the "Theology of the Body," delivered by Pope St. John Paul II between 1979 and 1984.

His reflections are based on Scripture and contain a vision of the human person truly worthy of man. Emphasizing the theme of love as self-gift, they counteract societal trends that view the body as an object of pleasure or as a machine for manipulation.

Instead, the [human] body shows us the call and gives us the means to love in the image of God....

John Paul II encourages a true reverence for the gift of our sexuality and challenges us to live it in a way worthy of our great dignity as human persons. His theology is not only for young adults and married couples, but for all ages and vocations, since it sums up the true meaning of being a person.[80]

In a beautiful section of Sacred Scripture, St. Paul exhorts the members of the Church at Corinth to glorify God in *both* body *and* spirit. In talking about the body here, he states in part: "Shun immorality. Every other sin which a man commits is outside the body; but the immoral man sins against his own body. Do you not know that your body is a temple of the Holy Spirit within you, which you have from God? You are not your own; you were bought with a price. So glorify God in your body." (1 Cor. 6:18–20)

Moral evils such as abortion, euthanasia, contraception, embryonic-stem-cell research, and human cloning all challenge the

---

[80] "What Is the Theology of the Body," Theologyofthebody.net.

innate dignity of the human person, as do unnatural marriage (in its multiple and varied forms), pornography, drug abuse, human trafficking, and the homeless crisis. Gender theory and transgender ideology promote metaphysical dualism and distort reality and the very order of creation itself.[81] But given the awesome truth of the body-soul composite of the human person and the dignity that lies therein, we do well to study the Church's—and Pope St. John Paul II's—"theology of the body," a theology that resonates with love, truth, goodness, and beauty.

[81] See Congregation for Catholic Education, *"Male and Female He Created Them": Towards a Path of Dialogue on the Question of Gender Theory in Education* (Vatican City: Congregation for Catholic Education, 2019).

Why It Is Wrong for a Man and Woman
to Live Together before Marriage

But immorality and all impurity or covetousness must not even be named
among you, as is fitting among saints. Let there be no filthiness, nor silly
talk, nor levity, which are not fitting; but instead let there be thanksgiving.
Be sure of this, that no immoral or impure man, or one who is covetous
(that is, an idolater), has any inheritance in the kingdom of Christ and of
God. Let no one deceive you with empty words, for it is because of these
things that the wrath of God comes upon the sons of disobedience.

—Ephesians 5:3-6

Inordinate love of the flesh is cruelty, because under the appearance of
pleasing the body, we kill the soul.

—St. Bernard of Clairvaux[82]

There's an old, wise maxim that goes something like this: "The
breaking of the rules before marriage will naturally lead to the
breaking of the rules after marriage." It has also been said, "fornication before marriage will likely lead to adultery after marriage." St.
Augustine, states: "The Apostle Paul tells us that the fruits of the
works of the flesh are: fornication, uncleanness, lust, idolatry, and

---

[82] Thigpen, *A Dictionary of Quotes from the Saints*, 90.

enmity. The fruits that will identify the good tree are: charity, joy, peace, benignity, faith, meekness, and continence."[83] St. Augustine, who himself suffered from a lust addiction for many years and tells us all about it in his famous *Confessions*, also says, "The freedom of the will is then true freedom when it does not serve vices and sins."[84]

But what if the couple is living chastely? What if the couple is not having premarital relations? Let's say they're living together chastely for the sake of cutting down on expenses—for the consolidating of bills—and that they're planning on getting married in the future. Is it then okay for them to live together before marriage, without the benefits of the marriage covenant? The answer is simply no, and this answer makes good, logical sense.

As faithful Catholics, we already know that the sin of fornication (sexual relations before marriage) is displeasing to Almighty God. And if done with full knowledge and deliberate consent, it is a mortal sin. But even in a chaste relationship, there is the question of all of the beautiful "mystery" that the marriage covenant brings with itself. If such mysteries (whether sexual or non-sexual) are all discovered before marriage, then the couple, once married, will begin their covenantal union with no foundation on which to build its success. The old adage, "familiarity breeds contempt," comes to mind here.

Even more, why would someone take the risk of putting himself or herself in a position to sin? In other words, why play by the edge of the cliff if you don't want to fall off the cliff? Remember: as Catholics, we know that we're called not only to avoid sin, but also to avoid what are called the "near occasions" of sin—those persons, places, or things that can lead us to sin. Living together—or *cohabitation*—puts one at grave risk of just that. To move in together is simply not a wise move at all, nor is it pleasing to Almighty God.

[83] Schroeder, *Every Day Is a Gift*, 23.
[84] Thigpen, *A Dictionary of Quotes from the Saints*, 92.

On Divorced Catholics Receiving the Sacraments of Confession and Eucharist

The woman answered him, "I have no husband." Jesus said to her, "You are right in saying, 'I have no husband'; for you have had five husbands, and the one you now have is not your husband; this you said truly."

—John 4:17–18

It is sometimes reported that a large number of Catholics today do not adhere to the teaching of the Church on a number of questions, notably sexual and conjugal morality, divorce and remarriage. Some are reported as not accepting the Church's clear position on abortion. It has also been noted that there is a tendency on the part of some Catholics to be selective in their adherence to the Church's moral teachings. It is sometimes claimed that dissent from the Magisterium is totally compatible with being a "good Catholic" and poses no obstacle to the reception of the sacraments. This is a grave error.

—Pope St. John Paul II[85]

---

[85] Address to the bishops of the United States, Minor Seminary of Our Lady of the Angels (Los Angeles), September 16, 1987, 5.

Whether or not they can go to Confession and receive the Eucharist faithfully and regularly is an important question for divorced Catholics—remarried or not—who wish to draw closer to Christ and His Church and partake of these sacraments in a worthy manner. The answer to this question is really quite simple: Yes, they can receive both sacraments, provided they have repented and are living chastely.

A divorced Catholic who is not remarried, so long as they are living a chaste life and not having a sexual relationship with someone who is not their lawful spouse, can go to Confession and receive Holy Communion at Mass. Likewise, a divorced-and-remarried Catholic who has remarried without having had their first marriage declared null by the Church, can also go to Confession and receive Holy Communion, provided they are living chastely with the person who is now their purely "civil" spouse. The phrase we hear applied to such cases is, "they live together as brother and sister"—in other words, with no conjugal relations and in perfect continence.

Indeed, there is an important difference between marriage in the eyes of the state (civil marriage) and marriage in the eyes of Holy Mother Church (sacramental marriage). This crucial difference naturally carries over to the reality of divorce. Simply put, a civil divorce puts into effect legally a claim that the indissoluble marriage bond validly entered into between a man and a woman is broken; yet, in the eyes of the Catholic Church, a civil divorce *does not* free persons from a valid (sacramental) marriage bond before Almighty God. Therefore, remarriage would not be morally licit unless the first marriage has been declared annulled—declared that it was never a sacrament to begin with.

Holy Mother Church wishes to reach out to divorced Catholics, whether remarried or not. The *Catechism* makes this clear in providing a nice summation and guide on this particular teaching:

Today there are numerous Catholics in many countries who have recourse to civil *divorce* and contract new civil unions. In fidelity to the words of Jesus Christ—"Whoever divorces his wife and marries another, commits adultery against her; and if she divorces her husband and marries another, she commits adultery"—the Church maintains that a new union cannot be recognized as valid, if the first marriage was. If the divorced are remarried civilly, they find themselves in a situation that objectively contravenes God's law. Consequently, they cannot receive Eucharistic communion as long as this situation persists. For the same reason, they cannot exercise certain ecclesial responsibilities. Reconciliation through the sacrament of Penance can be granted only to those who have repented for having violated the sign of the covenant and of fidelity to Christ, and who are committed to living in complete continence (CCC 1650).

There is another important point that must be mentioned, here. According to Church teaching: "It can happen that one of the spouses is the innocent victim of a divorce decreed by civil law; this spouse therefore has not contravened the moral law. There is a considerable difference between a spouse who has sincerely tried to be faithful to the sacrament of marriage and is *unjustly abandoned*, and one who through his *own grave fault* destroys a canonically valid marriage" (CCC 2386, emphasis added). In such cases, the petitioner of the divorce would have Holy Communion deferred until he or she repents of *having abandoned the innocent spouse*. This truth is intimated in CCC 1650 when it states clearly that, "reconciliation through the sacrament of Penance can be granted only to those who have repented for having violated the sign of the covenant and of fidelity to Christ, and who are committed to living in complete continence."

As a final point, here, it is very important to understand that our Lord Jesus Christ and His Bride, the Church, teach so clearly on this topic *precisely* because the sacramental covenant of marriage, against which divorce denigrates and militates, is the *very sign* of the *covenant of salvation*: "*Divorce* is a grave offense against the natural law. It claims to break the contract, to which the spouses freely consented, to live with each other till death. *Divorce does injury to the covenant of salvation, of which sacramental marriage is the sign.* Contracting a new union, even if it is recognized by civil law, adds to the gravity of the rupture: the remarried spouse is then in a situation of public and permanent adultery" (CCC 2384, emphasis added). Likewise, "divorce is immoral also because it introduces disorder into the family and into society. This disorder brings grave harm to the deserted spouse, to children traumatized by the separation of their parents and often torn between them, and because of its contagious effect which makes it truly a plague on society" (CCC 2385).

Parenthood as Rooted in the Fatherhood of God

I bow my knees before the Father, from whom every family in heaven and on earth is named.

—Ephesians 3:14–15

It is not enough for Christian parents to nourish only the bodies of their children; even the animals do this. They must also nourish their souls in grace, in virtue, and in God's holy commandments.

—St. Catherine of Siena[86]

In her teachings on marriage and family life, Holy Mother Church is clear to point out that human parenthood is deeply rooted in the divine fatherhood of Almighty God—so much so that divine fatherhood is said to be the very source of both human fatherhood and human motherhood. We see this teaching rooted in, for example, Eph. 3:14–15 wherein we read, "I bow my knees before the Father, from whom every family in heaven and on earth is named." And let's not forget that the Fourth Commandment tells us to "Honor thy father and mother."

[86] Schroeder, *Every Day Is a Gift*, 14.

The *Catechism* expresses this teaching clearly in CCC 239: While it is true that "God transcends the human distinction between the sexes"—that is, "He is neither man nor woman"—we still know that Jesus time and again refers to His *"Father"* in Heaven. In short, "no one is father as God is Father." "By calling God 'Father,' the language of faith indicates two main things: that God is the first origin of everything and transcendent authority; and that he is at the same time goodness and loving care for all his children." And while "God's parental tenderness can also be expressed by the image of motherhood, which emphasizes God's immanence, the intimacy between Creator and creature"; nevertheless, in the Gospels, Jesus always refers to His "Father" in Heaven.

So it is that the Church teaches that "the language of faith thus draws on the human experience of parents, who are in a way the first representatives of God for man." To sum this all up, while God "transcends human fatherhood and human motherhood," He "is their origin and standard." This is a wonderful truth to help fathers and mothers comprehend and appreciate their awesome role as parents: God's standard bearers on earth.

Duties of Parents

And he went down with them and came to Nazareth, and was
obedient to them; and his mother kept all these things in her heart.
And Jesus increased in wisdom and in stature, and in favor with God
and man.

—Luke 2:51–52

Catholic parents must learn to form their family as a "domestic
Church," a church in the home *as it were, where God is honored,*
his law is respected, prayer is a normal event, virtue is transmitted
by word and example, and everyone shares the hopes, the problems
and sufferings of everyone else. All this is not to advocate a return to
some outdated style of living: it is to return to the roots of human
development and human happiness!

—Pope St. John Paul II[87]

The important role of parents is foundational in the Church's
teaching on the sanctification of marriage and family life. In fact,
it is a doctrine that is part and parcel with the Church's theology

---

[87] Homily given at Aqueduct Racecourse, Brooklyn, New York, October 6, 1995, no. 7.

concerning the Sacrament of Matrimony. The *Catechism* beautifully articulates in detail the Church's full teaching on the duties of parents in paragraphs 2221–2231.

In short, parents are to provide for the physical and intellectual well-being of their children, but they are especially bound by divine law to educate their children for God and for eternal salvation. Vatican II, in its *Declaration on Christian Education*, states that it is the duty of parents to "create a family atmosphere inspired by love and respect for God and man, in which the well-rounded personal and social education of children is fostered."[88]

Because the Church views family life as an initiation into society, parents are called to contribute solidly to their children's moral education and spiritual formation, as well: "The fecundity of conjugal love cannot be reduced solely to the procreation of children, but must extend to their moral education and their spiritual formation. 'The *role of parents in education* is of such importance that it is almost impossible to provide an adequate substitute' "[89] (CCC 2221). In fact, the Church teaches that "the right and duty of parents to educate their children are primordial and inalienable" (CCC 2221). Moreover, parents must regard their children as children of God and respect them as human persons. "A child is not something *owed* to one, but is a *gift*. The 'supreme gift of marriage' is a human person" (CCC 2378).

Parents also have a duty to create a home environment that is suited for education in the virtues and for their growth in the child's life. Parents hold the "responsibility and privilege of *evangelizing their children*. Parents should initiate their children at an

[88] Second Vatican Council, Declaration on Christian Education *Gravissimum Educationis* (October 28, 1965), no. 3.
[89] *Gravissimum Educationis* 3.

early age into the mysteries of the faith of which they are the 'first heralds' for their children. They should associate them from their tenderest years with the life of the Church. A wholesome family life can foster interior dispositions that are a genuine preparation for a living faith and remain a support for it throughout one's life" (CCC 2225). In addition, "parents have the mission of teaching their children to pray and to discover their vocation as children of God" (CCC 2226). What important duties parents have—parents are commissioned, as it were, by Almighty God. Let us never forget this beautiful truth.

The Examination of Conscience

I always take pains to have a clear conscience toward God and toward men.

—Acts 24:16

This is our glory: the witness of our conscience. *There are men who rashly judge, who slander, whisper and murmur, who are eager to suspect what they do not see, and eager to spread abroad things they have not even a suspicion of. Against men of this sort, what defense is there save the witness of our own conscience?*

—St. Augustine[90]

A time-honored practice to help one prepare for a good, holy, and worthily received Sacrament of Penance is to make what is called an "examination of conscience," which is a prayerful self-reflection on our words and deeds in the light of the Gospel of Jesus Christ to determine how we may have sinned against God and neighbor. The *Catechism* states that the passages best suited for an examination of conscience before one receives the Sacrament of Penance

---

[90] *Sermo* 47, 12–14, *De ovibus*: CCL 41, 582–584, in *Liturgy of the Hours*, vol. III, 426.

can be found "in the Ten Commandments, the moral catechesis of the Gospels and the apostolic Letters, such as the Sermon on the Mount and the apostolic teachings" (CCC 1454). Most Catholic prayer books include a guide—typically listed in the Table of Contents—to help someone examine his conscience; also, examination of conscience brochures and leaflets often can be found in the vestibules of Catholic churches. With such tools—especially for those who partake of the Sacrament of Confession somewhat regularly—an examination of conscience should take no longer than ten to fifteen minutes.

In addition to specifically preparing for the Sacrament of Confession, there is also the time-honored practice of the *Particular* and the *General* examinations of conscience, which are two daily exercises that are of the utmost importance for those striving to advance in the spiritual life and in the way of perfection called for by our Lord. While each examination of conscience holds a long history in the devotional life of the Church, the two examens do differ.

With the *Particular Examen*, a person strives—usually around midday—to prayerfully examine his conscience in regard to some specific virtue he is trying to strengthen or some particular fault or vice he is trying to overcome. In this daily spiritual exercise, the focused-on virtue, fault, or vice of the *Particular Examen* is usually changed weekly or monthly.

With the *General Examen*, a person strives faithfully at the end of each day to look at that *entire* day with reference to any sins or faults committed and any virtues practiced. One's *General Examen*, then, provides a daily, thorough examination of conscience to determine whatever faults, failings, or sins that call for repentance might have been committed that day and whatever good actions might have been performed that day for which God should be thanked.

Both *Particular* and *General* examinations of conscience provide reflection, then, in God's presence, on the state of one's soul in two daily spiritual exercises that can be carried out in just three to five minutes each. Both examens should begin with a brief invocation for divine assistance and conclude with an act of contrition that can be from a favorite Catholic prayer book or simply uttered from the heart.

Indulgences

And he [Jesus] said to him, "Truly, I say to you, today you will be with me in Paradise."

—Luke 23:43

We are obliged to suffer in this life even after our sins have been pardoned, although original sin was the reason why we have fallen into this plight. For punishment lasts longer than sin so that sin is not regarded lightly, as would be the case were the punishment ended without the end of the sin. Thus, even when sin no longer holds us bound to eternal damnation, temporal punishment still is binding on us, either as a sign of the misery we have earned, as a corrective against a sinful life, or as an exercise in the patience we need.

—St. Augustine[91]

The Church's doctrine of indulgences is closely linked to the truth that there are four categorical consequences of sin: personal, social, ecclesial, and cosmic (see "Four Consequences of Personal Sin").

---

[91] In *Io. Ev. tract.* 124, 5; CCL 36, 683–684; PL 35 1972–1973, as quoted as a footnote in: *The Handbook of Indulgences: Norms and Grants* (New York: Catholic Book Publishing, 1991), 102.

While a valid sacramental Confession does grant to the penitent the forgiveness of sin, full restoration of communion with God, and therefore the remission of the *eternal* punishment of sin, *temporal* punishment still remains even after all guilt of the sin has been forgiven through the words of absolution imparted by the priest to the penitent. It is this temporal punishment that the doctrine of indulgences is about. Indulgences rid the soul of this temporal punishment either partially or fully.

As defined by the Church, an indulgence is "the remission before God of the temporal punishment due to sin whose guilt has already been forgiven. A properly disposed member of the Christian faithful can obtain an indulgence under prescribed conditions through the help of the Church which, as the minister of redemption, dispenses and applies with authority the treasury of the satisfactions of Christ and the saints. An indulgence is partial if it removes part of the temporal punishment due to sin, or plenary if it removes all punishment."[92] What a gift indulgences are! Look at it this way: Just as a husband might leave everything in his will to his wife to dispense of freely as she sees fit, so our Lord does so with His Bride, the Church. Remember, too, that indulgences can be applied to oneself (still living), or to a deceased person known or unknown to you. Indulgences cannot be applied to another living person, however, because a living person is still able to merit for himself.

The Church's *Handbook of Indulgences* is a real gem of a text to explain this doctrine further, and it can be obtained from your local Catholic bookstore or ordered online. It features the norms, grants, and conditions for obtaining a variety of Church-approved

---

[92] CCC glossary, s.v. "indulgence"; CCC 1471.

indulgences, from making the Sign of the Cross devoutly, to praying the Rosary, to visiting one of the patriarchal basilicas in Rome.

Never forget: Holy Mother Church, as the Bride of Christ, is the dispenser of the treasury won for us by her Bridegroom, Jesus Christ, on Calvary. Indulgences are a part of this wonderful treasury.

Divination

There shall not be found among you any one who burns his son or his daughter as an offering, any one who practices divination, a soothsayer, or an augur, or a sorcerer, or a charmer, or a medium, or a wizard, or a necromancer. For whoever does these things is an abomination to the Lord.

—Deuteronomy 18:10–12

Today it is up to you, brothers and sisters, following in the footsteps of those heroic and holy heralds of God, to offer the Risen Christ to your fellow citizens. So many of them are living in fear of spirits, of malign and threatening powers. In their bewilderment they end up even condemning street children and the elderly as alleged sorcerers. Who can go to them to proclaim that Christ has triumphed over death and all those occult powers? (see Ephesians 1:19–23; 6:10–12)

—Pope Benedict XVI[93]

Divination has traditionally been understood as "the art of knowing and declaring future events or hidden things by means of

[93] From a homily given at Saint Paul's Church in Luanda, Angola, March 21, 2009, during his Apostolic Journey to Cameroon and Angola.

communication with occult forces."[94] What's more, divination "is always an act of a religious nature. There is no divination if the religious element is missing, as in any scientific investigation."[95] This is precisely why "the occult forces in divination are always created rational powers that the Church identifies as diabolical."[96] Fr. Hardon states: "Implicit in this judgment is the belief that neither God nor the spiritual powers friendly to God would lend themselves to frivolous practices or subject themselves to any evoking human force. Hence, evoking these powers, whether explicitly or even implicitly, is considered an appeal to Satan's aid."[97] In short, "it is therefore a grave offense against God to attribute to the devil as sure knowledge of the contingent future, which, as depending on free will, is known to God alone."[98]

Based soundly on Sacred Scripture, Sacred Tradition, and the Magisterium, Church teaching on the subject of divination is clear. The *Catechism* states:

All forms of *divination* are to be rejected: recourse to Satan or demons, conjuring up the dead or other practices falsely supposed to "unveil" the future. Consulting horoscopes, astrology, palm reading, interpretation of omens and lots, the phenomena of clairvoyance, and recourse to mediums all conceal a desire for power over time, history, and, in the last analysis, other human beings, as well as a wish to conciliate hidden powers. They contradict the honor, respect, and loving fear that we owe to God alone." (CCC 2116)

[94] MCD, 162.
[95] MCD, 162–163.
[96] MCD, 163.
[97] MCD, 163.
[98] MCD, 163.

The soundness of this teaching explains the strong prohibitions in the Bible against any divination practices, such as that found in Leviticus 19:31, wherein we read: "Do not turn to mediums or wizards; do not seek them out, to be defiled by them: I am the Lord your God." The Church also teaches that "all practices of *magic* or *sorcery*, by which one attempts to tame occult powers, so as to place them at one's service and have a supernatural power over others—even if this were for the sake of restoring their health—are gravely contrary to the virtue of religion. These practices are even more to be condemned when accompanied by the intention of harming someone, or when they have recourse to the intervention of demons" (CCC 2117). In addition, "Wearing charms is also reprehensible. *Spiritism* often implies divination or magical practices; the Church for her part warns the faithful against it" (CCC 2117).

The *Catechism* states that "God can reveal the future to his prophets or to other saints. Still, a sound Christian attitude consists in putting oneself confidently into the hands of Providence for whatever concerns the future, and giving up all unhealthy curiosity about it" (CCC 2115). In the life of the faithful and solidly grounded Christian, then, all aspects of divination are to be avoided, since such grave practices clearly break the First Commandment: "I AM the Lord your God.... You shall have no other gods before me" (Exod. 20:2-3).

Superstition

But they had certain points of dispute with him about their own superstition and about one Jesus, who was dead, but whom Paul asserted to be alive.

—Acts 25:19

Science can purify religion from error and superstition; religion can purify science from idolatry and false absolutes. Each can draw the other into a wider world, a world in which both can flourish.

—Pope St. John Paul II[99]

Superstition is dangerous for the person who participates in any of its varied forms. It can lead one further into false devotion and go so far as to attribute magical powers to certain practices, objects, and creatures. Defined simply, superstition is the "unseemly or irreverent worship of God, or giving to a creature the worship that belongs to God."[100] The *Catechism* echoes this: "Superstition is the deviation of religious feeling and of the practices this feeling imposes. It can even

[99] Letter to Rev. George V. Coyne, S.J., former director of the Vatican Observatory, June 1, 1988.
[100] MCD, 526.

affect the worship we offer the true God, e.g., when one attributes an importance in some way magical to certain practices otherwise lawful or necessary. To attribute the efficacy of prayers or of sacramental signs to their mere external performance, apart from the interior dispositions that they demand, is to fall into superstition" (CCC 2111).

Fr. Hardon explains further that superstition "may stem either from false devotion or from a tendency toward magic. Giving divine worship to a creature is either idolatry, divination, or vain observance. The term 'superstition' more commonly means unbecoming worship to God."[101]

When it arises from false devotion, superstition "is really superfluous worship of God, which may take on a variety of forms. Their common denominator is an excessive concern that unless certain external practices, such as multiplication of prayers, are performed God will be displeased."[102] And "when superstition stems from a tendency toward magic, it reflects a false mentality that may or may not be the root of false devotion. Behind the false mentality is the notion that certain ritual practices, such as chain prayers or veneration of unapproved objects, carry with them an efficacy that is contrary to sound reason or the teaching of the Church."[103] Again, superstition attributes a kind of magical power to certain practices, objects, and creatures, such as chain letters, charms, or omens. Reliance on such power, rather than on trust in God, constitutes an offense against the honor, adoration, and worship due to Almighty God alone, as required by the First Commandment: "I AM the Lord your God.... You shall have no other gods before me" (Exod. 20:2-3).

[101] MCD, 526.
[102] MCD, 526.
[103] MCD, 526.

Scrupulosity

For godly grief produces a repentance that leads to salvation and brings no regret, but worldly grief produces death. For see what earnestness this godly grief has produced in you.

—2 Corinthians 7:10–11

Fly from scruples as from a pestilence; they make the soul lose immense treasures.

—St. Paul of the Cross[104]

If there is one thing to especially be on guard against as we experience growth in the spiritual life, it's scrupulosity. Fr. Hardon explains: Scrupulosity is "the habit of imagining sin where none exists, or grave [mortal] sin where the matter is venial."[105] A scrupulous conscience is "an erroneous conscience [that acts in such a way] when the mind is unduly swayed by fear and judges that something is wrong that in fact is lawful [or, at least *not* sinful]."[106] It's been said that scrupulosity in the spiritual life is a type of "religious

---

[104] Thigpen, *A Dictionary of Quotes from the Saints*, 206.
[105] MCD, 494.
[106] MCD, 494.

OCD" (obsessive compulsive disorder) or that scrupulous persons attempt to "make themselves their savior," thereby denying Jesus Christ that right. There is some truth in both of these descriptions, albeit unwittingly, on the part of the scrupulous person.

To understand a scrupulous conscience, it's important to know precisely what a "scruple" is. A scruple is an "unreasonable doubt about the morality of an act done or to be done. Its basis is an erroneous conscience combined with a lack of control of the emotion of fear."[107] The English word *scruple* comes from the Latin word *scrupulus*, which means a small, sharp stone or a small weight. In Latin, the word *scrupus* means rough stone. In other words, a scruple *pricks at* or *weighs heavy on* one's conscience, thus aggravating it.

Scrupulosity is real, but there is hope. Fr. Hardon advises, "To overcome scrupulosity, a person needs to be properly instructed in order to form a right conscience, and in extreme cases the only remedy is absolute obedience (for a time) to a prudent Confessor."[108] Also, there are several passages from Sacred Scripture that can help ease one's conscience and lead it toward renewal and recovery. For example, Revelation 21:5 gives the scrupulous person hope for renewal by reminding them of these words: "And he who sat upon the throne said, '*Behold, I make all things new.*' Also he said, 'Write this, for *these words are trustworthy and true.*'" Regarding recovering from scrupulosity and renewing one's trust in God for forgiveness as opposed to trusting in one's own efforts, Wisdom 7:27 can be applied. It states: "Though she is but one, she can *do all things*, and while remaining in herself, she *renews all things*; in every generation she *passes into holy souls* and makes them *friends of God.*"

---

[107] MCD, 494.
[108] MCD, 494.

Because true sorrow for actual sin and scrupulosity each bring their own respective grief to a person who is sincerely striving to advance in the spiritual life, it's very important to make a proper distinction between these two griefs. Words from 2 Corinthians 7:10-11 assist us in this regard. This Scripture passage states: "For godly grief produces a repentance that leads to salvation and brings no regret, but worldly grief produces death. For see what earnestness this godly grief has produced in you." In other words, scrupulosity brings with it the worldly grief that leads to death with no hope for forgiveness; whereas true repentance and sorrow for sin brings with it a godly grief in the form of sincere compunction of heart *with* hope for forgiveness. In the spiritual life, let us always strive for the latter.

Abortion, Artificial Contraception,
and Direct Sterilization

You shall not kill.

—Exodus 20:13

Among all the crimes which can be committed against life, procured abortion has characteristics making it particularly serious and deplorable. The Second Vatican Council defines abortion, together with infanticide, as an "unspeakable crime."

—Pope St. John Paul II[109]

The Church teaches that "human life must be respected and protected absolutely from the moment of conception. From the first moment of his existence, a human being must be recognized as having the rights of a person—among which is the inviolable right of every innocent being to life" (CCC 2270). What the *Catechism*

---

[109] Pope St. John Paul II, Encyclical *Evangelium Vitae* (March 25, 1995), no. 58, quoting Second Vatican Council, Pastoral Constitution on the Church in the Modern World *Gaudium et Spes* (December 7, 1965), no. 51.

is teaching us, here, is that the baby in utero is *not* a "potential human being" but rather a "human being with potential."

Indeed, "Since the first century the Church has affirmed the moral evil of every procured abortion. This teaching has not changed and *remains unchangeable*. Direct abortion, that is to say, abortion willed either as an end or a means, is gravely contrary to the moral law" (CCC 2271, emphasis added). The first-century Christian document known as the *Didache* [AD 70] states: "You shall not kill the embryo by abortion and shall not cause the newborn to perish."[110] And the Second Vatican Council—some two thousand years later—teaches, "God, the Lord of life, has conferred on men the surpassing ministry of safeguarding life in a manner which is worthy of man. Therefore from the moment of its conception life must be guarded with the greatest care while abortion and infanticide are unspeakable crimes."[111]

Formal cooperation in an abortion constitutes a grave offense against the moral law of God in what is objectively a mortal sin (see "Mortal Sin and Venial Sin" and "On Being an Accessory to Sin"). In fact, "The Church attaches the canonical penalty of excommunication to this crime against human life" (CCC 2272). The *Catechism*, quoting Canon Law (Canon 1398), states, "A person who procures a completed abortion incurs excommunication *latae sententiae*, by the very commission of the offense," and [is] "subject to the conditions provided by Canon Law" (CCC 2272). It is very important to know that, by means of this canonical penalty, "the Church does not thereby intend to restrict the scope of mercy. Rather, she makes clear the gravity of the crime committed, the

---

[110] *Didache* 2:1–2.

[111] *Gaudium et Spes* 51: "Abortus necnon infanticidium nefanda sunt crimina."

irreparable harm done to the innocent who is put to death, as well as to the parents and the whole of society" (CCC 2272; see "Four Consequences of Personal Sin"). Excommunication, therefore, is meant to be medicinal; it is not meant to be permanent. A person guilty of abortion (or a person who has cooperated willfully in an abortion) should take this sin to God's tribunal of mercy, the Sacrament of Confession, as soon as possible with true contrition. To guide us in this important teaching, let us remember what the Book of the Prophet Jeremiah (1:5) teaches us so beautifully: "Before I formed you in the womb I knew you, and before you were born I consecrated you." Almighty God knows *every* child in the womb.

Echoing this belief and teaching that God knows every child in the womb, Vatican II exhorts the following: "Let all be convinced that human life and the duty of transmitting it are not limited by the horizons of this life only: their true evaluation and full significance can be understood only in reference to *man's eternal destiny*"[112] (CCC 2371). What a beautiful truth. This is why artificial contraception and direct sterilization—like abortion—are considered intrinsically evil: " 'Every action which, whether in anticipation of the conjugal act, or in its accomplishment, or in the development of its natural consequences, proposes, whether as an end or as a means, to render procreation impossible'[113] is intrinsically evil" (CCC 2370).

Indeed, "periodic continence, that is, the methods of birth regulation based on self-observation and the use of infertile periods, is in conformity with the objective criteria of morality" (CCC 2370; cf. *Humanae Vitae* 16). This is because "these methods respect the bodies of the spouses, encourage tenderness between them, and

---

[112] *Gaudium et Spes* 51§4.

[113] Pope St. Paul VI, Encyclical *Humanae Vitae* (July 25, 1968), no. 14.

favor the education of an authentic freedom" (CCC 2370). But artificial contraception involves the "use of mechanical, chemical, or medical procedures [such as the tubal ligation of a female or the vasectomy of a male] to prevent conception from taking place as a result of sexual intercourse; contraception offends against the openness to procreation required of marriage and also the inner truth of conjugal love."[114] In short, the Church upholds these teachings *precisely* because "fecundity [fertility] is a good, a gift and an end of marriage. By giving life, spouses participate in God's fatherhood" (CCC 2398).

It should be noted that direct sterilization is not to be confused with indirect sterilization. Indirect sterilization is merely tolerated, not purposely sought out; for example, when a woman needs to have a hysterectomy because of uterine cancer or when a man must have a testicle removed (or receive high doses of radiation) because of testicular cancer. In such cases, the intention is not purposely to destroy a healthy and functioning reproductive organ to prevent the conception of children; rather, the intention is to remove or treat a diseased reproductive organ.

---

[114] CCC glossary, s.v. "contraception, artificial"; see CCC 2360-2379; 2392, 2394-2395, 2397, 2399.

Euthanasia

Do you not know that your body is a temple of the Holy Spirit within you, which you have from God? You are not your own.

— 1 Corinthians 6:19

I confirm that euthanasia is a grave violation of the law of God, since it is the deliberate and morally unacceptable killing of a human person. This doctrine is based upon the natural law and upon the written word of God, is transmitted by the Church's Tradition and taught by the ordinary and universal Magisterium.

— Pope St. John Paul II[115]

The Catholic Church teaches that direct euthanasia—whatever its motives and means—is "morally unacceptable" (CCC 2277) because it consists in purposely "putting an end to the lives of handicapped, sick, or dying persons" (CCC 2277). It has always been part of Catholic belief that "those whose lives are diminished or weakened deserve special respect. Sick or handicapped persons

---

[115] *Evangelium Vitae* 65, referencing Second Vatican Council, Dogmatic Constitution on the Church *Lumen Gentium* (November 21, 1964), no. 25.

should be helped to lead lives as normal as possible" (CCC 2276). Church teaching explains further:

> Thus an act or omission which, of itself or by intention, causes death in order to eliminate suffering constitutes a murder gravely contrary to the dignity of the human person and to the respect due to the living God, his Creator. The error of judgment into which one can fall in good faith does not change the nature of this murderous act, which must always be forbidden and excluded. (CCC 2277)

Human life is filled with difficulty, not least of which involves legitimate "end-of-life" healthcare decisions. Holy Mother Church understands this, and so she teaches the following with clarity:

> Discontinuing medical procedures that are burdensome, dangerous, *extraordinary*, or disproportionate to the expected outcome can be legitimate; it is the refusal of "over-zealous" treatment. Here one does not *will to cause death*; one's inability to impede it is merely accepted. The decisions should be made by the patient if he is competent and able or, if not, by those legally entitled to act for the patient, whose reasonable will and legitimate interests must always be respected. (CCC 2278, emphasis added)

Regarding elements that constitute *ordinary* care for the patient which can never be legitimately discontinued, the *Catechism* teaches:

> Even if death is thought imminent, the ordinary care owed to a sick person cannot be legitimately interrupted. The use of painkillers [e.g., morphine] to alleviate the sufferings of the dying, even at the risk of shortening their days,

can be morally in conformity with human dignity if *death is not willed as either an end or a means*, but only foreseen and tolerated as inevitable. Palliative care is a special form of disinterested charity. As such it should be encouraged. (CCC 2279, emphasis added)

Examples of palliative care would include such things as hydration; clean bed clothes and bedding; a regular moistening of the lips, mouth, and tongue; and the giving of nutrition that the body is still able to assimilate and process, whether given as a solid, liquid, or intravenously.

As a guide to help ensure that these *extraordinary* and *ordinary* care directives are carried out at a time when end-of-life issues need to be addressed, Catholic Christians should have in place a legally binding health care directive that is faithful to these norms and moral teachings of the Church, as well as someone legally designated as a medical proxy in case of incapacitation.[116]

Catholic moral teaching "reprobates euthanasia because it is a usurpation of God's lordship over human life. As creatures of God, to whom human beings owe every element of their existence, they are entrusted only with the stewardship of their earthy lives."[117] Indeed, all human persons "are bound to accept the life that God gave them, with its limitations and powers; to preserve this life as the first condition of their dependence on the Creator; and not deliberately curtail their time of probation on earth, during which they are to work out and thereby merit the happiness of their final destiny."[118]

---

[116] The National Catholic Bioethics Center offers the helpful publication *A Catholic Guide to End-of-Life Decisions*, https://www.ncbcenter.org/store/catholic-guide-to-end-of-life-decisions-english-pdf-download.
[117] MCD, 197.
[118] MCD, 197.

Suicide

When Judas, his betrayer, saw that he was condemned, he repented and brought back the thirty pieces of silver to the chief priests and the elders, saying, "I have sinned in betraying innocent blood." They said, "What is that to us? See to it yourself." And throwing down the pieces of silver in the temple, he departed; and he went and hanged himself.

—Matthew 27:3-5

If suicide is committed with the intention of setting an example, especially to the young, it also takes on the gravity of scandal.... Grave psychological disturbances, anguish, or grave fear of hardship, suffering, or torture can diminish the responsibility of the one committing suicide.

—CCC 2282

Objectively speaking, suicide is a mortal sin. It constitutes grave matter. *Subjectively* speaking, we just don't know. This is because we simply don't know "where the person was at psychologically" when they took their own life. For example, did the person have *fullness of will* in carrying out the suicidal act? (See "Mortal Sin and Venial Sin.") Again, we just don't know. So, *subjectively*, we leave the judgment to Almighty God. This is why the Church teaches that "we should not despair of the eternal salvation of persons who have taken their own lives" (CCC 2283). After all, "Grave psychological disturbances, anguish, or grave fear of hardship, suffering, or torture can diminish the responsibility of the one committing suicide" (CCC 2282). So it is, then, that the Church teaches that "by ways known to him alone, God can provide the opportunity for salutary repentance. The Church prays for persons who have taken their own lives" (CCC 2283).

These comforting truths, however, should never diminish the Christian teaching and truth that the act of suicide itself is gravely sinful. As explained in the *Catechism*: "Everyone is responsible for his life before God who has given it to him. It is God who remains the sovereign Master of life. We are obliged to accept life gratefully and preserve it for his honor and the salvation of our souls. We are stewards, not owners, of the life God has entrusted to us. It is not ours to dispose of" (CCC 2280).

In addition, "Suicide contradicts the natural inclination of the human being to preserve and perpetuate his life. It is gravely contrary to the just love of self. It likewise offends love of neighbor because it unjustly breaks the ties of solidarity with family, nation, and other human societies to which we have obligations. Suicide is contrary to love for the living God" (CCC 2281). Church teaching is also clear that "if suicide is committed with the intention of setting an example, especially to the young, it also takes on the gravity of scandal [see "On Giving Scandal to Others"]. Voluntary cooperation in suicide is contrary to the moral law" (CCC 2282). This is what makes practices like euthanasia and doctor-assisted suicide also gravely evil (see "On Being an Accessory to Sin").

Because it involves the "direct killing of oneself on one's own authority,"[119] suicide is a grave sin against both the natural and revealed law. Fr. Hardon explains further:

[119] MCD, 524.

Suicide offends against the divine precept "You shall not kill." One causes grave injury to the welfare of society [e.g., grave injury to one's family, friends, and other loved ones] and violates the virtue of charity to oneself. God is the supreme and exclusive owner of all things, so that exercising ownership over life is lawful only to God. He alone can take human life when he wills. The one who directly takes his or her own life violates the rights of God.[120]

We must always remember that God has created us to exist — to *be* — with Him forever in Heaven. If one commits suicide, he will still "exist" — but in a different state; that is, the afterlife. The question is: Where, ultimately? Heaven? Hell? Remember: the Particular Judgment is real, and it will be ratified at the General Judgment. So, while the earthly trials may be over for the one who commits suicide, his or her existence of *being* will *still continue to be* because of the immortality of the human soul, which will one day to be reunited with the body. Indeed, we must understand the *objectively* grave evil of suicide.

[120] MCD, 524.

Dogma

The Harmony of Faith and Reason

*We have not ceased to pray for you, asking that you may be filled with
the knowledge of his will in all spiritual wisdom and understanding,
to lead a life worthy of the Lord, fully pleasing to him, bearing fruit in
every good work and increasing in the knowledge of God.*

—Colossians 1:9–10

Faith opens the door to understanding, while unbelief closes it.

—St. Augustine, *Letter 137* to Volusian[121]

In the modern day and age in which we live, secular forces often
try to pit human faith against human reason, saying that the two
cannot co-exist within the same realm—for example, in the fields of
philosophy or science. As Christians, however, we know that nothing could be further from the truth. In fact, we believe firmly what
Pope St. John Paul II teaches: "Faith and reason are like two wings
on which the human spirit rises to the contemplation of truth."[122]

---

[121] *The Works of St. Augustine: A Translation for the 21st Century: Letters,*
ed. Boniface Ramsey, trans. Roland J. Teske, S.J., vol. 2 (Hyde
Park, NY: New City Press, 2003), 221.

[122] Pope St. John Paul II, Encyclical *Fides et Ratio* (September 14,
1998), prologue.

Simply put, faith and reason *are* harmonious. They must be. Why? Because both proceed from the same Author: God. Pope Benedict XVI rightly taught that whenever faith and reason part company, both become diseased. To give just two examples, history has shown that faith without reason can lead to religious fanaticism (for example, a nation declaring war in the name of religion); yet, reason without faith can lead to secularism, paganism, atheism, or any combination thereof. In short, "Benedict XVI has chosen to appeal to the language of intelligence to pluck at our heartstrings. He is aware that should one of the two 'wings'—faith and reason—be missing, the human soul is destined sooner or later to tumble into the abyss of desperation, nihilism and alienation."[123]

But in truth, the human person with his great gifts of reason and faith, represents the highest possibility the created order can attain. It is the human person who is capable of entering into a literal communion with God and God with him. The human person has this capacity because he is created in the *image* and *likeness* of God (Gen. 1:26–27). Many of the Church Fathers interpreted this passage from Scripture to mean that *image* refers to the human person's having both an intellect (the ability *to know*) and will (the ability *to choose*), while *likeness* refers to the human person's ability to partake of God's own divine life through (the reception of) sanctifying grace. Faith, therefore, is not an opponent of reason, but rather its true advocate. In fact, the Church teaches that God "can be known with certainty from the created world by the natural light of human reason" as the first principle and last end of all things (see CCC 36). Unfortunately, this truth is often

---

[123] Francesco M. Valiante, "On the Papacy of the Spiritual Director, Benedict XVI," EWTN, https://www.ewtn.com/catholicism/library/on-the-papacy-of-the-spiritual-director-benedict-xvi-1738.

obscured by the effects on our reason as a result of original sin; namely, a *darkened* intellect and a *weakened* will.

So, in defending the ability of human reason to know God, Holy Mother Church is expressing her confidence in the possibility of speaking about Him to all peoples of all cultures, thereby dialoguing with other religions, with philosophy and science, as well as with unbelievers, agnostics, and atheists.

Mercy Is Who God Is

But God, who is rich in mercy, out of the great love with which he loved us, even when we were dead through our trespasses, made us alive together with Christ.

—Ephesians 2:4–5

Before the Son of God became man, his goodness was hidden.... It was promised, but it was not experienced, and as a result few believed in it.... [But now] it is as if God the Father sent upon the earth a purse full of his mercy.... How could he have shown his mercy more clearly than by taking on himself our condition?... The incarnation teaches us how much God cares for us and what he thinks and feels about us.

—St. Bernard, Abbot[124]

A task given to each one of us baptized Christians is the proclamation of God's greatest attribute: His mercy. We are to proclaim it to everyone, both in our words and in the way we live our lives. Many of the Church Fathers referred to mercy as God's greatest attribute.

---

[124] *Sermo 1, in Epiphania Domini,* 1–2: PL 133, 141–143, in *Liturgy of the Hours,* vol. I, 446–447.

This is because Mercy is Who God is. It is "love's second name."[125] And this love does not falter or disappoint; the mercy and love of God are constant and ever-present for the asking. Regardless of one's sinful past, it is there to constantly guide and lead one on the road to sanctity. This is because God is more interested in our *future* than in our past. He is more interested in the kind of person *we can yet become* than in the kind of person we used to be.

God indeed takes our sins seriously. Whether venial or mortal, sins have in some way weakened or severed our supernatural relationship with Him. However, He never takes those sins as the last word, for three reasons: He is our God; He has made us in His image and likeness; and He is constantly calling us to Himself to live a life of sanctifying grace. Even more, God wants each one of us to become the *best versions* of ourselves: a version that already exists in His divine and ever-knowing mind. Since all knowledge is immediate to God's mind, that version has existed in God's mind eternally, even since before Creation. But to conform to this best version of self requires *conversion*, which involves a brutally honest reckoning with ourselves before God, and then working with God, Who is always ready to meet us where we are. St. Augustine describes this process aptly when he says, "God created us without us; but he did not will to save us without us."[126] So, let's work *with* God's mercy — and let His mercy work *in* and *through* us.

---

[125] Pope St. John Paul II, Encyclical *Dives in Misericordia* (November 30, 1980), no. 7.

[126] *Sermo* 169, 11, 13: *PL* 38, 923, as quoted in CCC 1847.

The Mercy of a Very Personal God

*But while he was yet at a distance, his father saw him and had
compassion, and ran and embraced him and kissed him.*

—Luke 15:20

*God's mercy is like an unleashed torrent. It bears away all hearts
in its flood.*

—St. John Marie Vianney[127]

It is one of the greatest acts of mercy that our very personal, loving, family-oriented, and Trinitarian God has revealed Himself
to all humanity. In the second divine personage of the Son, we
"see" God, and the Son, in turn, reveals to us His oneness with
the Father and the Holy Spirit. Maybe this is why Pope St. Leo
the Great says that through the sacred Incarnation, God enlarges
"our humanity without diminishing his divinity."[128]

---

[127] Quoted in Bert Ghezzi, *Voices of the Saints: A Year of Readings* (New
York: Doubleday, 2000), 599.

[128] *Epist.* 28 ad Flavianum, 3–4: PL 54, 763–767, in *Liturgy of the
Hours*, vol. II, 1746.

As an additional act of tremendous and loving mercy toward us, Almighty God has also given us the visible Church, the Bride of Christ, which we know by four distinctive marks: the fact that She is one, holy, catholic (universal), and apostolic. It is this Church—this Bride of Christ—that gives us the sacred deposit of faith: that "heritage of faith contained in sacred Scripture and Tradition, handed on in the Church from the time of the Apostles, from which the Magisterium draws all that it proposes for belief as being divinely revealed."[129]

Think about it: we literally can *know the truth* precisely because it *has been* revealed. We learn it, we give religious assent to it, we embrace it, and we share it with others. And this is all the result of—again—the mercy of a very personal, loving, family-oriented, Trinitarian God. All of these truths are wonders of His mercy that God wishes us to build our lives upon. Let's not miss them.

[129] CCC glossary, s.v. "deposit of faith"; see CCC 84, 1202.

God Offers Mercy before Justice

For judgment is without mercy to one who has shown no mercy; yet mercy triumphs over judgment.

—James 2:13

When we speak about wisdom, we are speaking of Christ. When we speak about virtue, we are speaking of Christ. When we speak about justice, we are speaking of Christ. When we speak about peace, we are speaking of Christ. When we speak about truth and life and redemption, we are speaking of Christ.

—St. Ambrose, Bishop and Doctor[130]

A strong theme of the Divine Mercy devotion is the fact that God wishes to offer His mercy *before* exercising His justice. This is seen time and again in St. Faustina's diary, *Divine Mercy in My Soul*. For example, our Lord tells her, "Write this: before I come as the just Judge, I am coming first as the King of Mercy."[131] He also says: "Before I come as a just Judge, I first open wide the door of

---

[130] *Ps.* 36, 65–66: CSEL 64, 123–125, in *Liturgy of the Hours*, vol. III, 216.
[131] *Diary* 83.

My mercy. He who refuses to pass through the door of My mercy must pass through the door of My justice."[132] Note the strong link between the latter quotation and John 10:7, wherein our Lord says, "I am the door." He beckons us to enter in and share a meal with him (think "Eucharist" here; see Rev. 3:20).

One of the most significant messages our Lord revealed to St. Faustina about His desire to extend His mercy before His justice to the repentant sinner is this: "Speak to the world about My mercy; let all mankind recognize My unfathomable mercy. It is a sign for the end times; after it will come the day of justice. While there is still time, let them have recourse to the fount of My mercy; let them profit from the Blood and Water which gushed forth for them"[133]

One last revelation worth sharing from St. Faustina's diary illustrates simply and lovingly the beautiful truth that Almighty God wishes to exercise toward *all* His mercy before His justice: "Before the Day of Justice, I am sending the Day of Mercy."[134] Amen to that. Let us not miss it; that day is *today* (see 2 Cor. 6:2).

---

[132] *Diary* 1146.
[133] *Diary* 848.
[134] *Diary* 1588.

God's Mercy and the End Times

Behold, now is the acceptable time; behold, now is the day of salvation.

—2 Corinthians 6:2

What is more equitable, what more true than that they should not themselves expect mercy from the judge, who themselves were unwilling to show mercy before the judge's coming. Those, however, who were willing to show mercy will be judged with mercy.

—St. Augustine[135]

Consider this paragraph from the *Catechism* that, at first glance, doesn't seem to have much to do with the mercy of God, but in reality, does:

> Before Christ's Second Coming the Church must pass through a final trial that will shake the faith of many believers (see Luke 18:8; Matt. 24:12). The persecution that accompanies her pilgrimage on earth (see Luke 21:12; John

---

[135] *Ps.* 95, 14. 15: CCL 39, 1351–1353, in *Liturgy of the Hours*, vol. IV, 536.

15:19–20) will unveil the *"mystery of iniquity"* in the form of a religious deception offering men an apparent solution to their problems at the price of apostasy from the truth. The supreme religious deception is that of the *Antichrist, a pseudo-messianism by which man glorifies himself in place of God and of His Messiah come in the flesh* (see 2 Thess. 2:4–12; 1 Thess. 5:2–3; 2 John 7; 1 John 2:18, 22). (675, emphasis added)

It is a wonderful act of mercy on God's part that He has revealed to us through Sacred Scripture, Sacred Tradition, and the Magisterium these truths regarding the end times. By knowing these truths, every generation can read its own "signs of the times" to avoid religious deception and apostasy from the truth so as to work out one's salvation with filial love of God and love of neighbor (see Phil. 2:12).

Our Lord Himself said to St. Faustina, the Divine Mercy seer, "Before I come as the just Judge, I am coming first as the King of Mercy."[136] And He also told St. Faustina—very directly in fact: "You will prepare the world for My final coming."[137]

Mercy calls us to the truth and shields us from destruction.

---

[136] *Diary* 83.
[137] *Diary* 429.

Church Discipline versus Doctrine, or Dogma

See to it that no one makes a prey of you by philosophy and empty deceit, according to human tradition, according to the elemental spirits of the universe, and not according to Christ.

—Colossians 2:8

The Church, which has spread everywhere, even to the ends of the earth, received the faith from the apostles and their disciples.... Having one soul and one heart, the Church holds this faith, preaches and teaches it consistently as though by a single voice. For though there are different languages, there is but one tradition. The faith and the tradition of the churches founded in Germany are no different from those founded among the Spanish and the Celts, in the East, in Egypt, in Libya and elsewhere in the Mediterranean world. Just as God's creature, the sun, is one and the same the world over, so also does the Church's preaching shine everywhere to enlighten all men who want to come to a knowledge of the truth.

—St. Irenaeus[138]

Simply put, Church discipline consists of those items upheld by the Church that *can* change. Doctrine, or dogma, on the other hand,

---

[138] *Lib.* 1, 10, 1–3: PG 7, 550–554, in *Liturgy of the Hours*, vol. II, 1784–1785.

according to the *Glossary* from the *Catechism of the Catholic Church*, are "the revealed teachings of Christ which are proclaimed by the fullest extent of the exercise of the authority of the Church's Magisterium. The faithful are obliged to believe the truths or dogmas contained in divine Revelation and defined by the Magisterium."[139] Doctrine *cannot* change.

For example, the Church's fasting laws and liturgical customs are considered disciplinary in nature—they *can* change. But Christ's bodily Resurrection and Ascension into Heaven and the Church's magisterial teaching on the evil of artificial contraception are clearly defined doctrines that cannot change. The same goes for the clearly defined dogmas of the Immaculate Conception and bodily Assumption of the Blessed Virgin Mary.

We know that doctrines and dogmas are to be upheld by all the faithful by way of one giving obedience of faith and religious assent (see CCC 891-892). But what about Church disciplines? The answer is simple: even though disciplines can change—say, over time and across cultures—those disciplines in effect "here and now" must be upheld and respected by the faithful, as the Church defines them by her legitimate teaching authority and teaching office, which we call the Magisterium.

---

[139] CCC glossary, s.v. "doctrine/dogma"; see CCC 88.

The Divinity of Jesus Christ

In the beginning was the Word, and the Word was with God, and the Word was God.

—John 1:1

[The Son of God] stooped down to take-up our lowliness without loss to his own glory. He remained what he was; he took-up what he was not. He wanted to join the very nature of a servant to that nature in which he is equal to God the Father. He wanted to unite both natures in an alliance so wonderful that the glory of the greater would not annihilate the lesser, nor the taking-up of the lower diminish the greatness of the higher.

—Pope St. Leo the Great[140]

Jesus Christ is one Person—a *divine* Person, because He is the Second Person of the Holy Trinity. But His one divine person-hood has two distinct and complete natures: divine *and* human. It is actually incorrect to say that Jesus Christ is a *human* person; rather, we say that He is a divine Person with a human nature—a

---

[140] *Sermo* 1 in Nativitate Domini, 2. 3: PL 54, 191–192, in *Liturgy of the Hours*, vol. III, 1539.

human nature, in fact, that is identical to our own in *every way* but sin (see Heb. 4:15).

Theologians use the phrase "hypostatic union" to describe the substantial unity of the divine and human natures in the one divine Person of Jesus Christ. *Hypostasis* in Greek refers to the substance or essential nature of an individual, so "hypostatic *union*" refers to the perfect, personal union of the two natures in Christ's divine Person; specifically, in the Second Divine Person of the Most Holy Trinity. This doctrine was proclaimed at the Council of Chalcedon in AD 451 and rightfully condemned two dangerous heresies: Nestorianism, which denied the *real unity* of the two natures of Christ's Person; and Monophysitism, which denied the *real distinction* between them. Thus the doctrine of the hypostatic union protects orthodox Christology against heterodox teachings that deny the substantial *unity* of the divine and human natures in Christ, or which, on the other hand, deny their *distinction*.

To sum this all up, then, Jesus Christ is one Person: a divine Person. He has two natures: a divine nature and a human nature. The Church believes that the divine and human natures remain distinct, and yet are perfectly united in Jesus Christ, the Second Person of the Most Holy Trinity and eternal Word of God.

The Resurrection of Jesus Christ

Jesus said to her, "I am the resurrection and the life; he who believes in me, though he die, yet shall he live, and whoever lives and believes in me shall never die. Do you believe this?"

—John 11:25-26

May your resurrection, Jesus, bring true greatness to our spiritual self and may your sacraments be the mirror wherein we may know that self.

—St. Ephrem[141]

Attributed to St. Augustine is the very eloquent saying, "The Resurrection of Christ was God's supreme and wholly marvelous work."[142] Indeed, the Church teaches that the Resurrection of Christ is the "crowning truth of our faith in Christ" (CCC 638).

Our Lord's Resurrection is the bodily rising of Jesus from the dead on the third day after His death on the Cross and burial in the tomb. Christ's Resurrection is a central truth of Christianity,

---

[141] *Sermo 3, de fine et admonitione,* 2. 4-5: ed. Lamy, 3, 216-222, in *Liturgy of the Hours,* vol. III, 1461.
[142] *Liturgy of the Hours,* vol. I, 1169.

which is expressed in all the Creeds and in all rules of faith of the early Church. As stated in the *Catechism* (639):

> The mystery of Christ's Resurrection is a real event, with manifestations that were historically verified, as the New Testament bears witness. In about AD 56, St. Paul could already write to the Corinthians, "I delivered to you as of first importance what I also received, that Christ died for our sins in accordance with the scriptures, and that he was buried, that he was raised on the third day in accordance with the scriptures, and that he appeared to Cephas, then to the Twelve ..." (1 Cor. 15:3-4). The Apostle speaks here of the living tradition of the Resurrection which he had learned about after his conversion at the gates of Damascus.

So it is, then, that the Resurrection of Jesus Christ from the dead truly is "the crowning truth of our faith in Christ, a faith believed and lived as the central truth by the first Christian community; handed on as fundamental by Tradition; established by the documents of the New Testament; and preached as an essential part of the Paschal mystery along with the cross" (CCC 638). St. Paul, in Acts 13:32-33, sums all of this up nicely when he says, "And we bring you the good news that what God promised to the fathers, this he has fulfilled to us their children by raising Jesus." Good News, indeed!

Private Revelation

So, every sound tree bears good fruit, but the bad tree bears evil fruit.
A sound tree cannot bear evil fruit, nor can a bad tree bear good fruit.

—Matthew 7:17–18

I prefer the monotony of obscure sacrifice to all ecstasies. To pick up a
pin for love can convert a soul.

—St. Thérèse of Lisieux[143]

St. Thomas Aquinas, the great Doctor of the Church, teaches that the purpose of private revelation is neither to prove Christian doctrine nor to add to Christian doctrine, but rather to offer people of a certain time in history a direction for human action; that is, to help people live out their faith more fully during the times in which they live. Some of these private revelations have been officially recognized by the authority of the Church, such as those of the Blessed Virgin Mary appearing at Lourdes, France, in 1858; at Fatima, Portugal, in 1917; and at Akita, Japan, in 1973. Private

---

[143] Quoted in Omer Englebert, *The Lives of the Saints*, trans. Christopher and Anne Fremantle (Lyndhurst, NJ: Barnes and Noble, 1994), 376.

revelations may occur as supernatural visions, as locutions (i.e., spoken words), or as divine touches (i.e., deep spiritual sentiments accompanied by a vivid illumination of the mind). Fr. Hardon notes that, "often, it is impossible to distinguish these three forms in practice, especially since they may be received simultaneously."[144]

As "supernatural manifestations by God of hidden truths made to private individuals for their own spiritual welfare or that of others,"[145] private revelations differ from the public revelation contained in Sacred Scripture and Tradition, which is given on behalf of the entire human race and which is necessary for human sanctification and salvation. "Although recognized by the Church and, at times, approved by her authority, private revelations are not the object of divine faith that binds one in conscience on God's authority."[146] The assent given to private revelations, therefore, is based either on merely human evidence or, whenever they are formally approved by the local bishop as worthy of belief or of supernatural origin, on ecclesiastical authority according to the mind of the Church. The Church cannot accept so-called private "revelations" that claim to surpass or correct the Revelation that Christ confided to His Church (see CCC 67).

[144] MCD, 441.
[145] MCD, 441.
[146] MCD, 441.

The Communion of Saints

Speaking the truth in love, we are to grow up in every way into him who is the head, into Christ, from whom the whole body, joined and knit together by every joint with which it is supplied, when each part is working properly, makes bodily growth and upbuilds itself in love.

—Ephesians 4:15–16

The communion of the saints. How shall I explain it to you? You know what blood transfusions can do for the body? Well, that's what the communion of the saints does for the soul.

—St. Josemaría Escrivá[147]

In Catholic teaching, the phrase "communion of saints" has two closely linked meanings: the communion existent "in holy things" and "among holy persons" (see CCC 946–948).

In regard to holy things, the Church refers to the whole communion of spiritual goods within the Church founded by Jesus Christ, which are readily made available to Her faithful members. These include a communion in the faith, a communion of the

---

[147] St. Josemaría Escriva, *The Way*, no. 544, Josemaría Escrivá, https://www.escrivaworks.org/book/the_way.htm.

sacraments, a communion of shared charisms granted by the Holy Spirit for the building-up of the Church, the sharing of material goods, and a communion rooted in charity. Among these spiritual goods and others, the Eucharist deserves special mention, for it is by the Eucharist—to quote Vatican II—that "the unity of all believers who form one body in Christ is both expressed and brought about."[148]

In regard to holy persons, the "three states of the Church" comprise the communion of saints: the members of the Church Triumphant in Heaven; the members of the Church Suffering in Purgatory, who are assured Heaven after their time of purification; and the members of the Church Militant on earth who are still living. The *Catechism* states, "In the communion of saints, 'a perennial link of charity exists between the faithful who have already reached their heavenly home, those who are expiating their sins in purgatory and those who are still pilgrims on earth'"[149] (CCC 1475).

To sum up, then, "We believe in the communion of all the faithful of Christ, those who are pilgrims on earth, the dead who are being purified, and the blessed in heaven, all together forming one Church; and we believe that in this communion the merciful love of God and His saints is always [attentive] to our prayers"[150] (CCC 962).

---

[148] *Lumen Gentium*, no. I.3.

[149] Pope Paul VI, Apostolic Letter *Indulgentiarum Doctrina* (January 1, 1967), 5.

[150] Pope St. Paul VI, Apostolic Letter *Solemni Hac Liturgia* (Credo of the People of God) (June 30, 1968), no. 30.

Antichrist

Children ... as you have heard that antichrist is coming, so now many antichrists have come.

—1 John 2:18

As in Christ dwells the fullness of the Godhead so in Antichrist the fullness of all wickedness. Not indeed in the sense that his humanity is to be assumed by the devil into unity of person ... but that the devil by suggestion infuses his wickedness more copiously into him than into all others. In this way all the wicked that have gone before are signs of Antichrist.

—St. Thomas Aquinas[151]

The Church teaches that the Antichrist is the chief of Christ's enemies. In both the First and Second Letters of St. John in the New Testament, he is named "Antichrist" specifically and is identified with unbelievers who deny the sacred Incarnation of Jesus Christ (see 1 John 2:18, 2:22, 4:3; and 2 John 7). According to Fr. Hardon, "Over the centuries, the Antichrist has been variously associated with historical persons" (e.g., the Roman Emperors

[151] *Summa Theologica*, III, q. 8, art. 8.

Caligula and Nero and the New Testament figure Simon Magus) or also with "organized movements such as Arianism. The more common Catholic interpretation says that he is not merely symbolic or an embodiment of the anti-Christian. The Antichrist is a real person."[152]

Given the fact that the senses of Scripture include both the literal and the spiritual, one could speculate indefinitely as to whether or not the Antichrist has already come, is in the world now, or has yet to come. The important point is that Catholic teaching states:

> Before Christ's second coming the Church must pass through a final trial that will shake the faith of many believers. The persecution that accompanies her pilgrimage on earth will unveil the "mystery of iniquity" in the form of a religious deception offering men an apparent solution to their problems at the price of apostasy from the truth. The supreme religious deception is that of the Antichrist, a pseudo-messianism by which man glorifies himself in place of God and of his Messiah come in the flesh. (CCC 675)

The Church also teaches that God's triumph over the revolt of evil prospered by the Antichrist and the spirit of Antichrist will take the form of the Last Judgment, after the final cosmic upheaval of this passing world. As the Creed succinctly teaches, "He will come again to judge the living and the dead." This excludes any prior coming of Christ, such as to set up an earthly kingdom. But, when He does return, for the one who is always faithful to God, there is nothing to fear.

---

[152] MCD, 29.

The Human Soul and Its Immortality

And do not fear those who kill the body but cannot kill the soul; rather fear him who can destroy both soul and body in hell.

—Matthew 10:28

He [God] gave him [man] a soul, made in his likeness, and endowed with memory, intellect and will; he gave him a body equipped with the senses; it was for him that he created heaven and earth and such an abundance of things. He made all these things out of love for man, so that all creation might serve man, and man in turn might love God out of gratitude for so many gifts.

—St. Alphonsus Liguori[153]

The human soul is the "spiritual principle of human beings. The soul is the subject of human consciousness and freedom."[154] The human soul is also the "spiritual immortal part in human beings that animates their body."[155] In Sacred Scripture, "the term 'soul' often refers to human *life* or the entire human *person*. But 'soul'

---

[153] *Tract. de praxis amandi Iesum Christum* edit. Latina, Romae, 1909, pp. 9–14, in *Liturgy of the Hours*, vol. IV, 1265.

[154] CCC glossary, s.v. "soul"; see CCC 363, 366, 1703.

[155] MCD, 513.

also refers to the innermost aspect of man, that which is of greatest value in him, that by which he is most especially in God's image: 'soul' signifies the *spiritual principle* in man" (CCC 363).

Also, the soul is made for union with the human body; in fact, this "unity of soul and body is so profound that one has to consider the soul to be the 'form' of the body" (CCC 365). In other words, "it is because of its spiritual soul that the body made of matter becomes a living, human body; spirit and matter, in man, are not two natures united, but rather their union forms a single nature" (CCC 365) that we properly call *human nature*. Important, too, is the truth that, "the Church teaches that every spiritual soul is created immediately by God—it is not 'produced' by the parents—and also that it is immortal; it does not perish when it separates from the body at death, and it will be reunited with the body at the final Resurrection" (CCC 366). At the Second Coming of Christ, then, the saved in Heaven and the damned in Hell will have their immortal souls reunited with their bodies for all eternity.

To sum up this teaching on the human soul, then, the *Catechism* teaches that "the human person, created in the image of God, is a being at once both physical and spiritual. The biblical account expresses this reality in symbolic language when it affirms that 'then the Lord God formed man of *dust from the ground* [the physical reality], and *breathed into his nostrils the breath of life* [the spiritual reality]; and man became a living being'" (CCC 362, emphasis added; quoting Gen. 2:7). The human person, whole and entire, and made up of physical and spiritual realities, is *willed by God*. In fact, "Of all visible creatures only man is 'able to know and love his creator'" (CCC 356); and "Endowed with 'a spiritual and immortal' soul, the human person is 'the only creature on earth that God has willed for its own sake.' From his conception, he is destined for eternal beatitude" (CCC 1703)—that is, the beatific vision—Heaven for all eternity.

The Four Last Things

But of that day and hour no one knows, not even the angels of heaven, nor the Son, but the Father only.

—Matthew 24:36

Judgment cannot be pronounced on a man until he has run his course of life.

—St. Thomas Aquinas[156]

The doctrine of the Four Last Things—death, judgment, Heaven, and Hell—is an important doctrine that no human person should take lightly. One day we shall die and be judged. Our eternity will either be one of salvation in Heaven with Christ and the saints, or it will be one of reprobation in Hell with the devils and the damned. The choice is ours to make.

The doctrine of the Four Last Things also means that there is no such thing as reincarnation; rather, immediately after death

---

[156] St. Thomas Aquinas, *The Summa Theologica*, trans. the Fathers of the English Dominican Province (New York: Benziger Bros., 1947), III, q. 59, art. 5.

each person is judged and receives his or her eternal destiny based on the living of their mortal life here on earth.

"Death puts an end to human life as the time open to either accepting or rejecting the divine grace manifested in Christ," and so "each man receives his eternal retribution in his immortal soul at the very moment of death, in a particular judgment that refers his life to Christ," with an entrance into Heaven, which can be either immediate or delayed by purification in Purgatory; or, with an entrance into Hell, which is immediate and everlasting (CCC 1021–1022). This teaching is clearly upheld by Sacred Scripture, Tradition, and the Magisterium.

The doctrine of the Four Last Things is not meant to frighten us. Rather, it is meant to lead us to live more faithful Christian lives here on earth. One meditation sums this up beautifully when it states:

> Death, judgment, Heaven and hell—these are the four last things toward which we are moving each hour of the day and night. They will never frighten us if our conscience is clear. If we love God in our daily life, that is, if we are sincerely trying to know and follow His holy Will, we have no reason to fear. By keeping this eternal goal ever before us, we shall think straight when life's problems and difficulties face us ... we must strive to become eternity-minded.[157]

[157] Fr. Anthony J. Paone, S.J., *My Daily Bread* (Charlotte, NC: TAN Books, 2014), introduction to bk. 1, pt. 1, sect. B.

Ecclesiology

The Church Has the Right and Duty to Call on the Mercy of God

If I am delayed, you may know how one ought to behave in the household of God, which is the church of the living God, the pillar and bulwark of the truth.

—1 Timothy 3:15

The Church is incapable of forgiving any sin without Christ, and Christ is unwilling to forgive any sin without the Church. The Church cannot forgive the sin of one who has not repented, who has not been touched by Christ; Christ will not forgive the sin of one who despises the Church.

—Bl. Isaac of Stella, Abbot[158]

In his landmark encyclical *Dives in Misericordia*, Pope St. John Paul II writes:

The Parable of the Prodigal Son [Luke 15:11–32] expresses in a simple but profound way the reality of conversion.

---

[158] *Sermo* 11: *PL* 194, 1728–1729, in *Liturgy of the Hours*, vol. IV, 246–247.

Conversion is the most concrete expression of the working of love and of the presence of mercy in the human world ... [and] the Church—professing mercy and remaining always faithful to it—*has the right and the duty to call upon the mercy of God*.... [Indeed] The Church must profess and proclaim God's mercy in all its truth, as it has been handed down to us by revelation.[159]

This is the heart of the message of God's mercy: the possibility of one's conversion and acceptance of God's love and forgiveness and the Church's right—as the Bride of Christ—to proclaim these to the modern world. Holy Mother Church, being just that—a good and holy mother—wants to guide her children to salvation.

Remember: God is always calling us to communion with Himself and is even willing to meet each person where they are in the life of faith. So respond, with your intellect and will, to God's merciful desire to have a relationship with you, and become enamored with the wonders of His mercy.

---

[159] *Dives in Misericordia* 6, 12, 13, emphasis added.

Holy Mother Church as a Field Hospital

*Those who are well have no need of a physician, but those who are
sick.*

—Matthew 9:12

*We always find that those who walked closest to Christ, our Lord,
were those who had to bear the greatest trials.*

—St. Teresa of Avila[160]

One of the most beautiful images of the Church that I have ever
come across is that of a "field hospital" during a time of combat or
war. Pope Francis first provided this analogy in his book entitled
The Name of God Is Mercy, and he used it in the context of sinners
who recognize themselves as such, and who need the mercy of God
in order to be forgiven and healed. In his book, the Holy Father
states the following:

> "The Church is called on to pour its mercy over all those
> who recognize themselves as sinners, who assume respon-
> sibility for the evil they have committed, and who feel in

---

[160] Thigpen, *A Dictionary of Quotes from the Saints*, 235.

need of forgiveness. The Church does not exist to condemn people but to bring about an encounter with the visceral love of God's mercy. I often say that in order for this to happen, it is necessary to go out.... I like to use the image of a field hospital to describe this 'Church that goes forth'; it exists where there is combat, it is not a solid structure with all the equipment where people go to receive treatment for both small and large infirmities. It is a mobile structure that offers first aid and immediate care, so that its soldiers do not die. It is a place for urgent care, not a place to see a specialist."[161]

Extending this theme of mercy and the Church's role in attending to the wounded, Pope Francis also states, "Mercy is the very foundation of the Church's life" and, "The Church has an endless desire to show mercy."[162]

Pope St. John Paul II echoes these truths when he states, "The Church lives an authentic life when she professes and proclaims mercy—the most stupendous attribute of the Creator and of the Redeemer—and when she brings people close to the sources of the Savior's mercy, of which she is the trustee and dispenser."[163]

That is Holy Mother Church: the Bride of Christ, the "field hospital," looking for the wounded to help them become forgiven and healed—and saved.

---

[161] *The Name of God Is Mercy*, 52–53.

[162] Pope Francis, Bull of Indiction of the Extraordinary Jubilee of Mercy *Misericordiae Vultus* (April 11, 2015), no. 10.

[163] *Dives in Misericordia* 15.

The Authority of Bishops in Union with the Pope

The saying is sure: If any one aspires to the office of bishop, he desires a noble task.

—1 Timothy 3:1

You have entered upon the office of bishop. Sitting at the helm of the Church, you pilot the ship against the waves. Take firm hold of the rudder of faith so that the severe storms of this world cannot disturb you. The sea is mighty and vast, but do not be afraid, for as Scripture says: he has founded it upon the seas, and established it upon the waters.

—St. Ambrose[164]

To understand the authority of bishops in union with the pope—which is foundational to the reality of the Church's "Magisterium," Her teaching authority—we have to look to the relationship that Jesus had with the twelve apostles. The *Catechism* says it best: "When Christ instituted the Twelve, 'he constituted [them] in the form of a college or permanent assembly, at the head of which

---

[164] *Epist.* 2, 1-2. 4-5. 7: *PL* (edit. 1845,) 879, 881, in *Liturgy of the Hours*, vol. I, 1218.

he placed Peter, chosen from among them.' Just as 'by the Lord's institution, St. Peter and the rest of the apostles constitute a single apostolic college, so in like fashion the Roman Pontiff, Peter's successor, and the bishops, the successors of the apostles, are *related with* and *united to* one another'"[165] (CCC 880, emphasis added).

Whenever we hear the phrase "college of bishops" or the "collegiality of bishops," this is in reference to the joint fellowship and authority enjoyed by all the bishops of the world in union with the Roman Pontiff. The successor of St. Peter himself, the Pope, who sits at the head of the college of bishops—the successors to the apostles—exercises supreme authority over the Church in teaching, governing, and sanctifying. Yet, the Pope is no mere member of this college, since "this power [of the college] cannot be exercised without the agreement of the Roman Pontiff" (CCC 883).

All of this helps us to see and understand the incredible history of and the absolute necessity for the Church's Magisterium, which, instituted by Christ Himself, ensures the Church's fidelity to the teaching of the apostles in matters of faith and morals and gives an authentic interpretation to the Word of God, whether in its written form of Sacred Scripture or in the oral form of handed-down tradition.

[165] *Lumen Gentium* 19 and 20.

Power of the Keys

And I tell you, you are Peter, and on this rock I will build my church,
and the powers of death shall not prevail against it. I will give you the
keys of the kingdom of heaven, and whatever you bind on earth shall be
bound in heaven, and whatever you loose on earth shall be loosed
in heaven.

—Matthew 16:18–19

That faith which Christ commended in the prince of the apostles remains
forever unshaken. And, just as Peter's faith in Christ endures, so does
Christ's foundation upon Peter. The structure of truth persists; blessed
Peter retains his rock-like strength and has not abandoned the helm of the
Church which he took over.

Peter is called the rock; he is declared to be the foundation; he is made
doorkeeper of the heavenly kingdom; he is made judge of what is to be
bound or loosed, and his judgments remain valid even in heaven; in these
various ways, he is assigned a rank above the others.

—Pope St. Leo the Great[166]

---

[166] *Sermo 3 de natali ipsius*, 2–3; PL 54, 145–146, in *Liturgy of the Hours*, vol. IV, 1754–1755.

The phrase "power of the keys" refers to the "ecclesiastical authority conferred by Christ on St. Peter and his successors."[167] The term is derived from Christ's promise to give Peter the keys of the kingdom of Heaven: "I will give you the keys of the kingdom of heaven, and whatever you bind on earth shall be bound in heaven, and whatever you loose on earth shall be loosed in heaven" (Matt. 16:19).

More broadly, however, the expression "power of the keys" refers to the Church's "exercise of authority to forgive or retain sins in the sacrament of penance."[168] After His Resurrection, Christ sent His apostles "that repentance and forgiveness of sins should be preached in his name to all nations" (Luke 24:47). "The apostles and their successors carry out this 'ministry of reconciliation,' not only by announcing to men God's forgiveness merited for us by Christ, and calling them to conversion and faith, but also by communicating to them the forgiveness of sins in Baptism, and reconciling them with God and with the Church through the 'power of the keys' received from Christ" (CCC 981).

The *Catechism* quotes St. Augustine, who states that the Church "has received the keys of the kingdom of heaven so that, in her, sins may be forgiven through Christ's blood and the Holy Spirit's action. In this Church, the soul dead through sin comes back to life in order to live with Christ, whose grace has saved us" (CCC 981). And the *Roman Catechism* states that, "There is no one, however wicked and guilty, who may not confidently hope for forgiveness, provided his repentance is honest."[169] Jesus Christ, Who died for all, desires that in His Church the gates of forgiveness should always be open to anyone who turns away from sin.

[167] MCD, 430.
[168] MCD, 430.
[169] *Roman Catechism* 1, 11, 5, as quoted in CCC 982.

Fathers of the Church

We have renounced disgraceful, underhanded ways; we refuse to practice cunning or to tamper with God's word, but by the open statement of the truth we would commend ourselves to every man's conscience in the sight of God.

—2 Corinthians 4:2

It will not be out of place to consider the ancient tradition, teaching and faith of the Catholic Church, which was revealed by the Lord, proclaimed by the apostles and guarded by the fathers. For upon this faith the Church is built, and if anyone were to lapse from it, he would no longer be a Christian either in fact or in name.

—St. Athanasius[170]

The phrase "Fathers of the Church" refers to those "Church teachers and writers of the early centuries whose teachings are a witness to the Tradition of the Church."[171] They are those holy writers of roughly the first-through-seventh centuries whom the

---

[170] *Ep.* 1 ad Serapionem 28–30: PG 26, 594–595. 599, in *Liturgy of the Hours*, vol. III, 584.

[171] CCC glossary, s.v. "Fathers of the Church"; see CCC 78, 688.

Church recognizes as her special witnesses of the faith. They are
called "Church Fathers" because of their "antiquity, orthodoxy,
sanctity and approval by the Church."[172] Many, though not all,
Fathers of the Church are canonized saints; many served as bishops, and some are even declared Doctors of the Church. Many
of the Church Fathers also answered heresies with writings that
gave rise to theological studies in their purity, while others helped
formulate the sacred liturgy and composed the basic professions
of faith found in the Nicene-Constantinopolitan and Athanasian
Creeds.

There are nearly one hundred Church Fathers, and they are
commonly divided into two categories that are at once both lin-
guistic and geographic: the Latin Fathers and Greek Fathers. It is
generally held that the last of the Western-Latin Fathers was St.
Isidore of Seville, who died in AD 636, and the last of the Eastern-
Greek Fathers was St. John Damascene, who died in AD 749.

By means of Tradition, "the Church through her doctrine,
life, and worship perpetuates and transmits to every generation
all that she is and all that she believes"[173] (CCC 78). The writings and teachings of the Fathers of the Church "are a witness to
the life-giving presence of this Tradition, showing how its riches
are poured out in the practice and life of the Church, in her
belief and her prayer" (CCC 78). So it is that the Fathers of the
Church are always timely witnesses to the Church's Tradition,
which is the living transmission of the message of the gospel in
the Church.

[172] MCD, 208.
[173] Second Vatican Council, Dogmatic Constitution on Divine Revelation *Dei Verbum* (November 18, 1965), no. 8.1.

Infallible and Magisterial Pronouncements of Faith and Morals

Having purified your souls by your obedience to the truth for a sincere love of the brethren, love one another earnestly from the heart. You have been born anew, not of perishable seed but of imperishable, through the living and abiding word of God.

—1 Peter 1:22–23

It is sometimes reported that a large number of Catholics today do not adhere to the teaching of the Church on a number of questions, notably sexual and conjugal morality, divorce and remarriage. Some are reported as not accepting the Church's clear position on abortion. It has also been noted that there is a tendency on the part of some Catholics to be selective in their adherence to the Church's moral teachings. It is sometimes claimed that dissent from the Magisterium is totally compatible with being a 'good Catholic' and poses no obstacle to the reception of the sacraments. This is a grave error.

—Pope St. John Paul II[174]

Catholics seem to know well that the Second Vatican Council had much to say about faith, morality, and obedience to Church

---

[174] Address to the bishops of the United States, Minor Seminary of Our Lady of the Angels (Los Angeles), September 16, 1987, 5.

teaching. After all, these are important components of the "univer-sal call to holiness" that help all members of the Church—bishops, priests, deacons, consecrated religious, and lay faithful—to sanctify themselves, others, the Church, and the world. However, two teachings of Vatican II somehow seem to have gotten lost in the shuffle during the years following the Council—doctrines which are *essential* to marking the road to sanctity for those who seek holi-ness. What are these two teachings? They are the moral obligation to give "obedience of faith" to all magisterial teachings infallibly proclaimed to be of divine and Catholic faith; and to give "religious assent" to all magisterial teachings, even if *not* infallibly proclaimed. Indeed, *all* members of the faithful—lay, religious, and cleric—are called to express this loyalty to the Church's Magisterium, Her teaching authority. Why are these teachings important? Because faith, obedience, and religion also function as individual virtues to be practiced and nurtured in the spiritual life.

Our Baptism and Confirmation call us to uphold *all* Church teaching, whether defined by the Magisterium as infallible or not. While infallible pronouncements—like the Immaculate Conception of the Blessed Virgin Mary or the bodily Resurrection of Christ—re-quire *obedience of faith*, all ordinary pronouncements—like the Church's teaching on the evil of artificial contraception—require *religious assent*. But both are just that: *required*. This is because religious assent, "though distinct from the assent [obedience] of faith, is nonetheless an extension of it."[175] As faithful sons and daughters of the Church—the Bride of Christ—we acknowledge obedience of faith and religious assent as two guides that assist us in working out our salvation (see Phil. 2:12).

[175] For more on this teaching, read CCC 888-892.

The Four Marks of the Church

Husbands, love your wives, as Christ loved the church and gave himself up for her, that he might sanctify her, having cleansed her by the washing of water with the word, that he might present the church to himself in splendor, without spot or wrinkle or any such thing, that she might be holy and without blemish.

—Ephesians 5:25–27

I believe in one, holy, catholic and apostolic Church...

—Nicene-Constantinopolitan Creed, AD 325

The four marks of the Church are those characteristics that authenticate the one true Church founded by Jesus Christ; namely, the fact that His Church is one, holy, catholic, and apostolic. We profess our belief in these four marks each Sunday at Mass when we pray the Nicene-Constantinopolitan Creed. Vatican II teaches that "this is the one Church of Christ, which in the Creed is professed as one, holy, catholic and apostolic."[176] These four characteristics are inseparably linked with each other and indicate essential features of the Church and Her mission. But the Church

---

[176] *Lumen Gentium* 8.

does not possess these marks of Herself; rather, "it is Christ who, through the Holy Spirit, makes his Church one, holy, catholic, and apostolic, and it is he who calls her to realize each of these qualities" (CCC 811). And while these four marks are recognized by faith, they also "speak clearly to human reason" (CCC 812). To describe these marks briefly (see CCC 866-870):

- When we say that the Church is "one," we mean that Her members are united in faith; they believe the same doctrines, receive the same sacraments, and are united under the Pope, the Vicar of Christ on earth—the Successor of St. Peter: "one Lord, one faith, one baptism" (see Eph. 4:5).

- When we say that the Church is "holy," we mean that God is Her very author and that She is God-centered. Her teachings come from Jesus Christ, Her life is animated by the Holy Spirit, and all Her members—though sinners—are called to loving union with the Father. The Church's holiness shines in the lives of the saints.

- When we say that the Church is "catholic"—which means "universal"—we believe that She was founded by Jesus Christ for all peoples of every time and place and that She teaches to all nations—in the fullness of the Faith—the doctrines of Her Bridegroom and Lord. All of this makes the Church missionary by nature.

- And when we say that the Church is "apostolic," we mean that She alone teaches entire the doctrines of Christ that have been handed down by Him to the apostles, and from the apostles to their successors, the bishops. This fact upholds the Church infallibly in the truth.

For a fuller treatment of these four marks of the Church, read the *Catechism of the Catholic Church*, paragraphs 811-865.

Baptismal Priesthood and Ministerial Priesthood

You are a chosen race, a royal priesthood, a holy nation, God's own people, that you may declare the wonderful deeds of him who called you out of darkness into his marvelous light.

—1 Peter 2:9

Listen now to what the Apostle urges us to do. I appeal to you, he says, to present your bodies as a living sacrifice. *By this exhortation of his, Paul has raised all men to priestly status.*

How marvelous is the priesthood of the Christian, for he is both the victim that is offered on his own behalf, and the priest who makes the offering. He does not need to go beyond himself to seek what he is to immolate to God: with himself and in himself he brings the sacrifice he is to offer God for himself. The victim remains and the priest remains, always one and the same. Immolated, the victim still lives: the priest who immolates cannot kill. Truly it is an amazing sacrifice in which a body is offered without being slain and blood is offered without being shed. ...

Let your heart be an altar. Then, with full confidence in God, present your body for sacrifice. God desires not death, but faith; God thirsts not for blood, but for self-surrender; God is appeased not by slaughter, but by the offering of your free will.

—St. Peter Chrysologus[177]

---

[177] *Sermo* 108: *PL* 52, 499–500, in *Liturgy of the Hours*, vol. II, 771–772.

In Catholic theology, all the baptized faithful participate in the one priesthood of Jesus Christ in either or both of two ways: the *baptismal priesthood*, also referred to as the common priesthood of all the faithful, or the common priesthood of all the baptized, and which is received through the Sacrament of Baptism; and the *ministerial priesthood*, also called the hierarchical priesthood, which is received through the Sacrament of Holy Orders and which is reserved to men alone (see "Priestly Ordination Reserved to Men Alone"). Unfortunately, these two distinct participations in Christ's one priesthood often become convoluted: for example, at the parish level, duties strictly intended for the priest are sometimes assumed by the laity, and those strictly intended for the laity are often assumed by the priest. This blurring of participatory distinction can lead to those phenomena referred to as the "clericalization of the laity" and the "laicization of the clergy."[178]

Based solidly on Scripture, Tradition, and the Magisterium, Church teaching on this topic is clear. The *Catechism* states:

> The ministerial or hierarchical priesthood of bishops and priests, and the common priesthood of all the faithful participate, "each in its own proper way, in the one priesthood of Christ." While being ordered "one to another," they differ essentially. In what sense? While the common priesthood of the faithful is exercised *by* the unfolding of baptismal grace ... the ministerial priesthood is at the service of the common priesthood. It is directed *at* the

[178] See Pope St. John Paul II, Post-synodal Apostolic Exhortation *Christifideles Laici* (December 30, 1988), no. 23; see also the address of Pope St. John Paul II to the bishops of the Antilles on their Ad Limina visit, May 7, 2002.

unfolding of the baptismal grace of all Christians. (CCC 1547, emphasis added)

As Catholics, we hold that the ministerial priesthood, through the power of the laying on of hands from a bishop, who is a direct descendent of the apostles, is "a *means* by which Christ unceasingly builds up and leads his Church" (CCC 1547) in its common priesthood of all the faithful. This is why the ministerial priesthood has its own sacrament, that of Holy Orders. And through the Sacraments of Baptism and Confirmation, the faithful exercise their common priesthood—each according to his or her own vocation—through their participation in Christ's own mission as priest, prophet, and king (see CCC 897, 901-911). This is something that the ministerial priesthood does as well in its own proper way. Indeed, what a gift the Church has in these two priesthoods. As it is a priest who offers sacrifice to almighty God, this is precisely why the laity are able to have these words addressed to them at Mass by the priest celebrant: "Pray, brethren (brothers and sisters), that my sacrifice and yours may be acceptable to God, the almighty Father."[179]

---

[179] *The Roman Missal*, English translation according to the Third Typical Edition (Totowa, NJ: Catholic Book Publishing, 2011), 382, emphasis added.

Priestly Ordination Reserved to Men Alone

And he called to him his twelve disciples and gave them authority over unclean spirits, to cast them out, and to heal every disease and every infirmity. The names of the twelve apostles are these: first, Simon, who is called Peter, and Andrew his brother; James the son of Zebedee, and John his brother; Philip and Bartholomew; Thomas and Matthew the tax collector; James the son of Alphaeus, and Thaddaeus; Simon the Cananaean, and Judas Iscariot, who betrayed him.

—Matthew 10:1-4

Although the teaching that priestly ordination is to be reserved to men alone has been preserved by the constant and universal Tradition of the Church and firmly taught by the Magisterium in its more recent documents, at the present time in some places it is nonetheless considered still open to debate, or the Church's judgment that women are not to be admitted to ordination is considered to have a merely disciplinary force.

Wherefore, in order that all doubt may be removed regarding a matter of great importance, a matter which pertains to the Church's divine constitution itself, in virtue of my ministry of confirming the brethren (cf. Lk 22:32) I declare that the Church has no authority whatsoever to confer priestly ordination on women and that this judgment is to be definitively held by all the Church's faithful.

—Pope St. John Paul II[180]

If there's one doctrinal teaching of the Catholic Church that particularly stands out in this modern day and age—a teaching that everyone, both Catholics and non-Catholics alike, seems to know, whether they agree with it or not—it is the teaching that priestly ordination is reserved to men alone.

Despite the many claims to the contrary, this time-honored doctrine, held by the Church since the time of Christ and His apostles, in no way militates against the dignity of women, their natural gifts, or their vocations. Nor is the fact that women are ineligible to receive the Sacrament of Holy Orders to be viewed as a limitation on their universal call to holiness or as a limitation or stifling of the baptismal priesthood that baptized women already share in.

In modern times, the Church has repeatedly and definitively reiterated the reasons why the Sacrament of Holy Orders can be received only by men. For example, Pope St. John Paul II quotes Pope St. Paul VI in stating some of these reasons, including "the example recorded in the sacred Scriptures of Christ choosing his apostles only from among men; the constant practice of the Church, which has imitated Christ in choosing only men; and her living teaching authority, which has consistently held that the exclusion of women from the priesthood is in accordance with God's plan for his Church."[181]

---

[180] Pope St. John Paul II, Apostolic Letter *Ordinatio Sacerdotalis* (May 22, 1994), no. 4.
[181] *Ordinatio Sacerdotalis* 1.

In actual fact, then, the Church concludes that She is not *authorized* to admit women to priestly ordination.[182] In other words, the Church Herself cannot change this teaching; She does not have the authority to do so. This is because the Church recognizes Herself *to be bound* by this choice made by the Lord Himself, a choice which He made *freely*, since He shows Himself time and time again in the Gospels to *not* have been subject to the prevailing customs or social conditions of His time.

[182] *Ordinatio Sacerdotalis* 2.

The Precepts of the Church

*Jesus said to them, "Truly, truly, I say to you, unless you eat the flesh
of the Son of man and drink his blood, you have no life in you."*

—John 6:53

*Let us then follow Christ's paths which he has revealed to us, above
all the path of humility, which he himself became for us. He showed
us that path by his precepts, and he himself followed it by his suffering
on our behalf.*

—St. Augustine[183]

The precepts of the Church, as defined by the *Catechism*, are those
positive laws or commandments "made by Church authorities to
guarantee for the faithful the indispensable minimum in prayer
and moral effort, for the sake of their growth in love of God and
neighbor."[184] These precepts "are set in the context of a moral life
bound to and nourished by liturgical life" (CCC 2041). Simply
put, since Holy Mother Church cares genuinely for Her children

---

[183] *Sermo* 23A, 1–4: CCL 41, 321–323, in *Liturgy of the Hours*, vol.
IV, 189.
[184] CCC glossary, s.v. "Precepts of the Church"; see CCC 2041.

and their spiritual growth, She sees to it that through legitimate Church authority, certain minimum requirements must be met so as to help ensure one's growth in love of God, of neighbor, and in the spiritual life.

The universal *Catechism* (2042-2043) lists the formal precepts for the Catholic Church's members; they are:

- "You shall attend Mass on Sundays and on holy days of obligation and rest from servile labor."
- "You shall confess your sins at least once a year."
- "You shall receive the sacrament of the Eucharist at least during the Easter season."
- "You shall observe the days of fasting and abstinence established by the Church."
- "You shall help to provide for the needs of the Church."

Rather than look upon the five precepts of the Church as some rigorous code to which we are bound under pain of sin, we should instead identify them for what they really are: guides given to us by Holy Mother Church—just as any good parent would guide their children—to ensure our advancement in a life of prayer and moral virtue, and growth in love of God and neighbor.

As Catholics, we should rejoice that our faith gives us simple, direct, and concrete guides—precepts—which function as sure norms to aid us as members of the Body of Christ to strive for holiness and to live our lives as God intends.

Obligatory Mass on Sundays and Holy Days

Remember the sabbath day, to keep it holy. Six days you shall labor, and do all your work; but the seventh day is a sabbath to the Lord your God.

—Exodus 20:8–10

By his resurrection he [our Lord] consecrated Sunday, or the Lord's day. Though the third after his passion, this day is the eighth after the Sabbath, and thus also the first day of the week.

—St. Augustine[185]

Sundays and holy days require obligatory Mass attendance by the Catholic Christian. Why? Not because we fear punishment from God if we don't go (i.e., servile fear); but precisely because we love Him (i.e., filial fear). Vatican II teaches, "the sacred liturgy is above all things the worship of the Divine Majesty."[186] God calls us to Himself, and we respond with sacred worship. Apart from illness,

---

[185] *Sermo* 8 in octava Paschae 1, 4: PL 46, 838. 841, in *Liturgy of the Hours*, vol. II, 636.

[186] Second Vatican Council, Constitution on the Sacred Liturgy *Sacrosanctum Concilium* (December 4, 1963), no. 33.

for example, the Church teaches that the faithful are obliged to participate in the celebration of the sacred liturgy on all Sundays and holy days of obligation. This is a grave obligation, and to willfully neglect it is itself a mortal sin that does merit eternal punishment if it is not confessed. In fact, every Sunday is a holy day of obligation. The *Code of Canon Law* (1246) states clearly that, "Sunday, on which by apostolic tradition the paschal mystery is celebrated, is to be observed in the universal Church as the primary holy day of obligation."

Other examples of holy days of obligation (apart from Sunday itself) include the solemnity of Mary, Mother of God, on January 1; the Immaculate Conception of the Blessed Virgin on December 8 and the Nativity of Our Lord on December 25. While there are other holy days of obligation established throughout the world, such as the Ascension of Our Lord on the fortieth day after Easter; the Assumption of the Blessed Virgin Mary on August 15, and the solemnity of All Saints on November 1, national bishops' conferences can dispense the faithful from the obligation for a just reason and even transfer a holy day to be observed on a Sunday.

As faithful sons and daughters of the Church, let us remember, too, that faithfully attending Mass on Sundays and holy days of obligation is not only an observance of the Third Commandment, but also a faithful adherence to a formal precept of the Church.

Interreligious Communion—Why Not?

Whoever, therefore, eats the bread or drinks the cup of the Lord in
an unworthy manner will be guilty of profaning the body and blood
of the Lord. Let a man examine himself, and so eat of the bread and
drink of the cup. For any one who eats and drinks without discerning
the body eats and drinks judgment upon himself.

—1 Corinthians 11:27-29

As sons of the light of truth, flee divisions and evil doctrines;
where your shepherd is, follow him as his flock....
   Be careful, therefore, to take part only in the one eucharist; for
there is only one flesh of our Lord Jesus Christ and one cup to unite
us with his blood, one altar and one bishop with the presbyters and
deacons, who are his fellow servants. Then, whatever you do, you will
do according to God.

—St. Ignatius of Antioch[187]

The Catholic Church does not permit interreligious Communion because we *believe in* and hold as *supremely precious* the

---

[187] *Letter to the Philadelphians*, 1, 1-2, 1; 3, 2-5: Funk 1, 226-229, in
Liturgy of the Hours, vol. IV, 360-361.

doctrine of Christ's Real Presence in the Eucharist—a doctrine that other Christian faiths do not hold—that is, the doctrine of transubstantiation.

We often hear the phrases "Communion" or "Holy Communion," referring to the reception of the Blessed Sacrament at Mass. But we need to stop and ponder what, exactly, these phrases mean. To receive *Communion* implies just that: a "communion," or joining, of faith in the Real Presence of Christ in the Eucharist in His Body, Blood, Soul, and Divinity. To receive *Holy* Communion implies that the person is partaking of something set apart by, and unto, God. This Holy Communion is effected both between the person and Christ and among *all* those who—as a single body—receive Christ in the Eucharist.

A statement from the United States Catholic Conference of Bishops explains all of this well: "Because Catholics believe that the celebration of the Eucharist is a sign of the reality of the oneness of faith, life and worship, members of those churches with whom we are not yet fully united are ordinarily not admitted to Holy Communion. Eucharistic sharing in exceptional circumstances by other Christians requires permission according to the directives of the diocesan bishop and the provisions of canon law."[188] Keep in mind, too, that a Catholic is *not* free to take part in a Protestant communion service. Such an action would imply a "communion" that simply does not exist, but for which we pray.

So, while we Catholics are not able to invite our non-Catholic Christian brothers and sisters to receive the Eucharist, we can

---

[188] United States Conference of Catholic Bishops (USCCB), "Guidelines for the Reception of Communion," https://www.usccb.org/prayer-and-worship/the-mass/order-of-mass/liturgy-of-the-eucharist/guidelines-for-the-reception-of-communion.

surely invite them to attend the celebration of holy Mass. We pray that our common baptism and the action of the Holy Spirit in the celebration of the Eucharist will draw us closer to one another and begin to dispel the sad divisions which separate us, keeping with Christ's prayer for us "that they may all be one" (John 17:21).

Importance of the Religious Habit

You are Christ's; and Christ is God's.

—1 Corinthians 3:23

The religious habit, an outward mark of consecration to God, should be simple and modest, poor and at the same becoming. In addition it must meet the requirements of health and be suited to the circumstances of time and place and to the needs of the ministry involved.

—*Perfectae Caritatis*[189]

Consecrated men and women belonging to the Church's many institutes of consecrated life and societies of apostolic life have, throughout the centuries, contributed to the Church's life of prayer and apostolic works. But it is not only the prayer and work of consecrated persons that has made the presence of the Church felt in the modern world of any age. The religious habit worn by consecrated Religious throughout the centuries has also played an important role in making the Church "visible" across the globe. Even today, there's something magnetic and special about witnessing, for

[189] Second Vatican Council, Decree on the Adaptation and Renewal of Religious Life *Perfectae Caritatis* (October 28, 1965), no. 17.

Catholic Essentials

example, a friar priest or a veiled nun in full habit at the airport or shopping for their communities at the local supermarket. This is testimony to the fact that the "Church visible" *means something.* The Church's very visibility helps to "make Christ present in the modern world" amidst the hustle and bustle of everyday activity.

Several Church documents have addressed the importance of the religious habit—most notably Vatican II's *Decree on the Adaptation and Renewal of Religious Life* (*Perfectae Caritatis*, October 28, 1965), and *Vita Consecrata*, Pope St. John Paul II's Post-Synodal Apostolic Exhortation on the *Consecrated Life and Its Mission in the Church and in the World* (March 25, 1996). In these teachings we learn, for example, that the religious habit is a sign of consecration in a particular religious community. It is "an outward mark of consecration to God, [it] should be simple and modest, poor and at the same becoming. In addition, it must meet the requirements of health and be suited to the circumstances of time and place and to the needs of the ministry involved."[190] In *Vita Consecrata*, Pope St. John Paul II states:

> Since the habit is a sign of consecration, poverty and membership in a particular Religious family, I join the Fathers of the Synod in strongly recommending to men and women religious that they wear their proper habit, suitably adapted to the conditions of time and place. Where valid reasons of their apostolate call for it, Religious, in conformity with the norms of their Institute, may also dress in a simple and modest manner, with an appropriate symbol, in such a way that *their consecration is recognizable.* Institutes which from their origin or by provision of their Constitutions do not

[190] *Perfectae Caritatis* 17.

have a specific habit should ensure that the dress of their members *corresponds in dignity and simplicity to the nature of their vocation.*"[191]

What a beautiful and becoming sign the religious habit is! It not only makes visible Christ and His Bride, the Church, in the midst of the modern world, but also makes visible one's consecration to Almighty God in their having professed the evangelical counsels of poverty, chastity, and obedience. And it also identifies the reality that a particular apostolate carried out by a particular institute—approved by the Church—has been founded by a founder or foundress who was truly inspired by the Holy Spirit for *that* particular work.

[191] Pope St. John Paul II, Post-synodal Apostolic Exhortation *Vita Consecrata* (March 25, 1996), no. 25, emphasis added.

The Church's Social Teaching

But if any one has the world's goods and sees his brother in need, yet closes his heart against him, how does God's love abide in him? Little children, let us not love in word or speech but in deed and in truth.

— 1 John 3:17-18

If you want Peace, work for Justice.

— Pope St. Paul VI[192]

Just as the Church has contributed greatly over the centuries to education and health care, the same can be said about Her social teaching—the social doctrine of the Church concerning the truths about human dignity and solidarity and the principles of human work, justice, and peace. The Church maintains a vested interest in these areas precisely because She "receives from the Gospel the full revelation of the truth about man" (CCC 2419). According to the *Catechism*: "'Christian revelation ... promotes deeper understanding of the laws of social living.'... When she [the Church] fulfills her mission of proclaiming the Gospel, she bears witness to man, in the name of Christ, to his dignity and his vocation to the

---

[192] Message for the Celebration of the Day of Peace, January 1, 1972.

communion of persons. She teaches him the demands of justice and peace in conformity with divine wisdom"[193] (CCC 2419). In short, "The Church makes a moral judgment about economic and social matters, 'when the fundamental rights of the person or the salvation of souls requires it' "[194] (CCC 2420).

The social doctrine of the Church developed especially during the nineteenth century, "when the Gospel encountered modern industrial society with its new structures for the production of consumer goods, its new concept of society, the state and authority, and its new forms of labor and ownership. The development of the doctrine of the Church on economic and social matters attests the permanent value of the Church's teaching at the same time as it attests the true meaning of her Tradition, always living and active"[195] (CCC 2421). Rooted in the Gospel, then, the Church's social teaching is timeless. It "comprises a body of doctrine, which is articulated as the Church interprets events in the course of history, with the assistance of the Holy Spirit, in the light of the whole of what has been revealed by Jesus Christ. This teaching can be more easily accepted by men of good will, the more the faithful let themselves be guided by it" (CCC 2422).

Within Her social doctrine, the Church does admit that "in the moral order she bears a mission distinct from that of political authorities: the Church is concerned with the temporal aspects of the common good because they are ordered to the sovereign Good, our ultimate end [God]. She strives to inspire right attitudes with respect to earthly goods and in socio-economic relationships"

---

[193] *Gaudium et Spes* 23 § 1.
[194] *Gaudium et Spes* 76 § 5.
[195] Pope St. John Paul II, Encyclical *Centesimus Annus* (May 1, 1991), no. 3.

(CCC 2420). For example, in more modern times the Church "has rejected the totalitarian and atheistic ideologies associated with 'communism' and 'socialism'" (CCC 2425) precisely because these systems militate against the rights of workers; for example, the right to form labor unions or other associations that help secure their rights to fair wages and to safe and humane working conditions. In Her social teaching, the Church "has likewise refused to accept, in the practice of 'capitalism,' individualism and the absolute primacy of the law of the marketplace over human labor" (CCC 2425).

Overall, the Church's social teaching "proposes principles for reflection; it provides criteria for judgment; it gives guidelines for action" (CCC 2423). For example: "Any system in which social relationships are determined entirely by economic factors is contrary to the nature of the human person and his acts"[196] (CCC 2423). Also, "A theory that makes profit the exclusive norm and ultimate end of economic activity is morally unacceptable. The disordered desire for money cannot but produce perverse effects. It is one of the causes of the many conflicts which disturb the social order"[197] (CCC 2424). And, likewise, "A system that 'subordinates the basic rights of individuals and of groups to the collective organization of production' is contrary to human dignity. Every practice that reduces persons to nothing more than a means of profit enslaves man, leads to idolizing money, and contributes to the spread of atheism. 'You cannot serve both God and mammon'"[198] (CCC 2424). Indeed, we possess a great gift in the Church's social teaching, as it protects the innate dignity of the human person.

[196] *Centesimus Annus* 24.
[197] Reference to *Gaudium et Spes*, 63 § 3; Pope St. John Paul II, On Human Work *Laborem Exercens* (September 14, 1981), no. 7, 20; *Centesimus Annus* 35.
[198] *Gaudium et Spes* 65 § 2; Matt. 6:24 and Luke 16:13.

Sacraments

The Seven Sacraments and Their Normative Frequency

Then Jesus came from Galilee to the Jordan to John, to be baptized by him. ... And when Jesus was baptized, he went up immediately from the water, and behold, the heavens were opened and he saw the Spirit of God descending like a dove, and alighting on him; and lo, a voice from heaven, saying, "This is my beloved Son, with whom I am well pleased."

—Matthew 3:13, 16-17

Enjoy the fragrance of eternal life, breathed on you by means of the sacraments.

—St. Ambrose[199]

According to the Church's teaching, how often should we normally receive the seven sacraments? Three of the sacraments can be received only once, because of their "spiritual character" and because of the "indelible mark" they leave on the Christian soul, never to be erased. These three sacraments are Baptism, Confirmation,

---

[199] From the beginning of the treatise *On the Mysteries*, Nn. 1-7: SC 25 bis, 156-158, in *Liturgy of the Hours*, vol. III, 483.

and Holy Orders. Two of the sacraments, that is, Confession and Eucharist, can be received *both* repetitiously (that is, "again and again") and frequently—even daily if you want them, provided, of course, it is not scrupulosity that is leading one to daily Confession. In this regard, scrupulosity may be defined as seeing sin where there is no sin or seeing mortal sin where, in reality, it is only venial sin (see "Scrupulosity").

The remaining sacraments, Matrimony and the Anointing of the Sick, can be received repetitiously but *not* frequently. In other words, they can indeed be received "again" (for example, if your spouse dies, you can remarry), but they're *not* received daily. The Anointing of the Sick can be received whenever one begins to be in danger of death because of sickness or old age. And for those in a persistent state of illness—with cancer, for example—the Anointing of the Sick can be received monthly. It can also be received again, whenever one's health condition worsens.

Rooted deeply in Sacred Scripture, let us remember that each sacrament is "an efficacious sign of grace, instituted by Christ and entrusted to the Church, by which divine life is dispensed to us through the work of the Holy Spirit."[200] I remember my Sacramental Theology professor at seminary teaching us men that each sacrament, when worthily received, is "a literal meeting with Lord Jesus." In other words, it is the mystery of *Christ made present*—and with the Eucharist, it is a literal meeting *par excellence* precisely because of Christ's Real Presence in the Eucharist: Body, Blood, Soul, and Divinity.

---

[200] CCC glossary, s.v. "sacrament"; see CCC 774, 1131, 1210.

St. Thomas Aquinas and the Eucharist

And he took bread, and when he had given thanks he broke it and gave it to them, saying, "This is my body which is given for you. Do this in remembrance of me."

—Luke 22:19

The Eucharist is, as it were, the consummation of the spiritual life, and the end of all the sacraments.

—St. Thomas Aquinas[201]

St. Thomas Aquinas is one of the greatest saints in the two-thousand-year history of the Catholic Church — and one who staunchly defended the doctrine of transubstantiation regarding our Lord's Real Presence in the Eucharist.

Born in 1225, Thomas was an Italian Dominican friar, Catholic priest, philosopher, and pre-eminent theologian. Today, he is a Doctor of the Church and patron saint of students and universities. His great work, the *Summa Theologica*, is considered paramount in Catholic philosophical and theological studies. When in 1264 Pope Urban IV added to the Church's liturgical calendar the Solemnity

---

[201] *Summa Theologica*, III, q. 73, art. 3.

of Corpus Christi, St. Thomas composed the liturgical texts for that new Mass, including its prayers and hymns.

Two well-known liturgical hymns that come from St. Thomas' Corpus Christi compositions are "O Salutaris Hostia" and "Tantum Ergo." These are comprised of stanzas from longer hymns written for Corpus Christi. "O Salutaris Hostia" reminds us of the glory of Heaven that awaits those who remain faithful to the saving Victim, our Eucharistic Lord and King, Jesus Christ, Who opens wide the gates of Heaven to us here below. In "Tantum Ergo," we sing of the doctrine of transubstantiation, defending the truth that "what our senses fail to fathom, let us grasp through faith's consent." Throughout the centuries, preeminent composers like Bach and Mozart have set these great Eucharistic hymns to music.

St. Thomas identified the goal of human existence as eternal union and eternal fellowship with God.[202] This is attained in the Beatific Vision—eternal beatitude and eternal life in Heaven. The Eucharistic hymns of St. Thomas Aquinas, including "Panis Angelicus" and "Pange Lingua Gloriosi," still aid the Church in her language of worship and devotion of the most Holy Eucharist—what Vatican II calls the "source and summit of the Christian life."[203] And it is through the Eucharist that "we have a foretaste of eternal life."[204]

---

[202] See *Summa Theologica*, I, II, q. 3, arts. 1–8.

[203] *Lumen Gentium* 11; CCC 1324.

[204] *Compendium of the Catechism of the Catholic Church* 274; see CCC 1090, 1326 (cf. 1 Cor. 15:28); *Sacrosanctum Concilium* 8; *Lumen Gentium* 50.

The Sacrificial Lamb and the Eucharist

Then I looked, and I heard around the throne and the living creatures and the elders the voice of many angels, numbering myriads of myriads and thousands of thousands, saying with a loud voice, "Worthy is the Lamb who was slain, to receive power and wealth and wisdom and might and honor and glory and blessing!"

— Revelation 5:11–12

If you desire further proof of the power of this blood, remember where it came from, how it ran down from the cross, flowing from the Master's side. The gospel records that when Christ was dead, but still hung on the cross, a soldier came and pierced his side with a lance and immediately there poured out water and blood. Now the water was a symbol of baptism and the blood, of the holy eucharist. The soldier pierced the Lord's side, he breached the wall of the sacred temple, and I have found the treasure and made it my own. So also with the lamb: the Jews sacrificed the victim and I have been saved by it.

— St. John Chrysostom[205]

---

[205] Cat. 3, 13–19: SC 50, 174–177, in *Liturgy of the Hours*, vol. II, 474.

The lamb is one of the most prominent and celebrated symbols of our Lord and Savior, Jesus Christ. Mentioned in both the Old Testament and New Testament numerous times, it is seen time and again as a *type* or *symbol* of Jesus Christ. For example, in the Gospel of St. John, Jesus is identified as "the Lamb of God who takes away the sin of the world" (John 1:29). According to Fr. Hardon, the lamb has been:

> Rendered in many forms as early as the fourth century. Various aspects show the animal balancing a staff by its right front leg, with a wound in its chest pouring blood into a chalice, representing Christ's Blood in the Passion; the staff bearing a flag signifying Christ's victory in the Resurrection; the lamb resting or standing on a closed book with its seven sealed streamers symbolizing Christ as the judge.[206]

Worth noting, here, is that some have interpreted these seven streamers to be symbolic, also, of the seven sacraments that Christ instituted in the Church and the book being symbolic of the Roman Missal used at Mass and which is placed upon the altar. And regarding that prominent symbol of the sacrificial lamb shown "balancing a staff by its right front leg, with a wound in its chest pouring blood into a chalice, representing Christ's Blood in the Passion," this particular image of the Lamb is directly tied to Christ and the Eucharist. As the *Catechism* teaches us:

> Christ's death is both the *Paschal sacrifice* that accomplishes the definitive redemption of men, through "the Lamb of God, Who takes away the sin of the world," and the *sacrifice of the New Covenant*, which restores man to communion

[206] MCD, 307.

with God by reconciling him to God through the "blood of the covenant, which was poured out for many for the forgiveness of sins." (CCC 613)

This sacrifice of Christ is unique; it completes and surpasses all other sacrifices. First, it is a gift from God the Father Himself, for the Father handed His Son over to sinners in order to reconcile us with Himself. At the same time, it is the offering of the Son of God made man, who in freedom and love, offered His life to His Father through the Holy Spirit in reparation for our disobedience. (CCC 614)

Let us love the sacrificial Lamb, our Lord and Savior Jesus Christ, Who is really, truly, and substantially present in the Most Holy Eucharist.

The Lamb as an Emblem of Docility

He was oppressed, and he was afflicted, yet he opened not his mouth;
like a lamb that is led to the slaughter, and like a sheep that before its
shearers is dumb, so he opened not his mouth.

—Isaiah 53:7

Why a lamb in his passion? Because he underwent death without
being guilty of any iniquity.

—St. Augustine[207]

In Sacred Scripture, the lamb is viewed as an "emblem of docility."[208]
In Isaiah 53, for example, we read about the Suffering Servant—a
type or image of Jesus. We are told that although "He was oppressed, and he was afflicted, yet he opened not his mouth; like
a lamb that is led to the slaughter, and like a sheep that before its
shearers is dumb, so he opened not his mouth" (v. 7).

This imagery has strong ties to Good Friday, when Jesus was
led to Golgotha, carrying His Cross, and offered Himself to the
Father in the Holy Spirit for the salvation of the world. "The

---

[207] *The Works of St. Augustine*, 330.
[208] MCD, 307.

perfect sacrifice was Christ's death on the cross; by this sacrifice, Christ accomplished our redemption as high priest of the new and eternal covenant. The sacrifice of Christ on the cross is commemorated and mysteriously made present in the Eucharistic sacrifice of the Church"[209] through which our Lord becomes really, truly, and substantially present in the most Holy Eucharist in His Body, Blood, Soul, and Divinity. All of this reveals the truth that from the greatest of sufferings, trials, and tribulations comes the greatest of gifts that renews, sustains, and saves: the Eucharist—the "source and summit of the Christian life,"[210] the "foretaste of eternal life."[211]

St. Teresa Benedicta of the Cross, the Carmelite martyr who died at Auschwitz, understood this truth. Well aware of the evils of World War II that were raging outside the cloister walls, she said:

> Just as the Lamb had to be killed to be raised upon the throne of glory, so the path to glory leads through suffering and the Cross for everyone chosen to attend the marriage supper of the Lamb. All who want to be married to the Lamb must allow themselves to be fastened to the Cross with Him. Everyone marked by the blood of the Lamb is called to this, and that means all the baptized.... The fountain from the heart of the Lamb has not dried up. We can wash our robes clean in it even today as the thief on Golgotha once did. Trusting in the atoning power of this

[209] CCC glossary, s.v. "sacrifice"; see CCC 616, 1357, 1544, 1545, 2099.
[210] *Lumen Gentium* 11; CCC 1324.
[211] *Compendium of the Catechism of the Catholic Church* 274.

holy fountain, we prostrate ourselves before the throne of the Lamb and answer His question: "Lord, to whom shall we go? You have the words of eternal life (John 6:68)."[212]

---

[212] St. Teresa Benedicta of the Cross, *The Hidden Life: Essays, Meditations, Spiritual Texts*, ed. Dr. L. Gelber and Michael Linssen, O.C.D., trans. Waltraut Stein, Ph.D. (Washington, D.C.: ICS Publications, Institute of Carmelite Studies,1992), 99, 101.

The Presence of Christ and the Real Presence of Christ in the Eucharist

*Now as they were eating, Jesus took bread, and blessed, and broke
it, and gave it to the disciples and said, "Take, eat; this is my body."
And he took a cup, and when he had given thanks he gave it to them,
saying, "Drink of it, all of you; for this is my blood of the covenant,
which is poured out for many for the forgiveness of sins."*

—Matthew 26:26–28

*What more could Jesus have done for us? Truly, in the Eucharist, he
shows us a love which goes "to the end" (see John 13:1), a love which
knows no measure.*

—Pope St. John Paul II[213]

Vatican II has much to say about the presence of Jesus Christ in the
sacred liturgy. For example, the *Sacrosanctum Concilium* 7 tells us:

> Christ is always present in His Church, especially in her
> liturgical celebrations. He is present in the sacrifice of the

---

[213] Pope St. John Paul II, Encyclical *Ecclesia de Eucharistia* (April 17,
2003), no. 11.

Mass, not only in the person of His minister, "the same now offering, through the ministry of priests, who formerly offered himself on the cross," but especially under the Eucharistic species. By His power He is present in the sacraments, so that when a man baptizes it is really Christ Himself who baptizes. He is present in His word, since it is He Himself who speaks when the holy scriptures are read in the Church. He is present, lastly, when the Church prays and sings, for He promised: "Where two or three are gathered together in my name, there am I in the midst of them" (Matt. 18:20).

In the passage above from Vatican II, the words "but especially under the Eucharistic species" mean something special and profound. To echo what this is, exactly, the *Catechism* states, beautifully:

The mode of Christ's presence under the Eucharistic species is *unique*. It raises the Eucharist above all the sacraments as "the perfection of the spiritual life and *the end to which all the sacraments tend*." In the most blessed sacrament of the Eucharist, "the body and blood, together with the soul and divinity, of our Lord Jesus Christ and, therefore, *the whole Christ, is truly, really, and substantially contained*. This presence is called 'real' — by which is not intended to exclude the other types of presence as if they could not be 'real' too, but because it is *presence in the fullest sense*: that is to say, it is a *substantial presence* by which Christ, God and man, makes himself *wholly* and *entirely* present." (CCC 1374, emphasis added)

In other words, whereas the other six sacraments "effect what they signify," the Eucharist *is* what it signifies: Christ Himself really, truly, and substantially present in His Body, Blood, Soul and Divinity.

Transubstantiation

The cup of blessing which we bless, is it not a participation in the blood of Christ? The bread which we break, is it not a participation in the body of Christ?

—1 Corinthians 10:16

The Council of Trent summarizes the Catholic faith by declaring: "Because Christ our Redeemer said that it was truly his body that he was offering under the species of bread, it has always been the conviction of the Church of God, and this holy Council now declares again, that by the consecration of the bread and wine there takes place a change of the whole substance of the bread into the substance of the body of Christ our Lord and of the whole substance of the wine into the substance of his blood. This change the holy Catholic Church has fittingly and properly called transubstantiation."

—CCC 1376

Transubstantiation is the "scholastic term used to designate the unique change of Eucharistic bread and wine into the Body and Blood of Christ. 'Transubstantiation' indicates that through the consecration of the bread and the wine [by a validly ordained priest of the Church] there occurs the change of the entire substance of the bread into the substance of the Body of Christ, and of the entire substance of the wine into [the substance of] the Blood of Christ—even though the appearances or 'species' of bread and wine remain."[214] And while "the faith behind the term was already believed in apostolic times, the term itself [transubstantiation] was a later development."[215]

The Church Fathers throughout the early centuries "strongly affirmed the faith of the Church in the efficacy of the Word of Christ and of the action of the Holy Spirit to bring about this conversion" (CCC 1375). And the sixteenth-century Council of Trent teaches:

> Because Christ our Redeemer said that it was truly his Body that he was offering under the appearance of bread, it has *always* been the conviction of the Church of God, and this holy Council now declares *again*, that by the consecration of the bread and wine there takes place a change of the whole substance of the bread into the substance of the Body of Christ our Lord, and of the whole substance of the wine into the substance of his Blood. This change the holy Catholic Church has fittingly and properly called transubstantiation.[216]

Indeed, in the most Blessed Sacrament of the Eucharist "the body and blood, together with the soul and divinity, of our Lord Jesus Christ and, therefore, *the whole Christ, is truly, really, and substantially* contained" (CCC 1374). It is important to remember, too, as stated earlier (see "The Presence of Christ and the Real Presence of Christ in the Eucharist" and "The Phrase 'Blessed Sacrament'"), that this "mode of Christ's presence in the Eucharistic species is unique [among all the sacraments].... It raises the Eucharist above all the sacraments as "the perfection of the spiritual life and the end to which all the sacraments tend" (CCC 1374).

---

[214] CCC glossary, s.v. "transubstantiation"; see CCC 1376.

[215] MCD, 545.

[216] 13th Session, chap. IV, and quoted in CCC 1376.

The Phrase "Blessed Sacrament"

I am the living bread which came down from heaven; if any one eats
of this bread, he will live for ever; and the bread which I shall give for
the life of the world is my flesh.

—John 6:51

The visit to the Blessed Sacrament ... is a great treasure of the Catholic
faith. It nourishes social love and gives us opportunities for adoration
and thanksgiving, for reparation and supplication. Benediction of the
Blessed Sacrament, Exposition and Adoration of the Blessed Sacrament,
Holy Hours and Eucharistic processions are likewise precious elements
... in full accord with the teaching of the Second Vatican Council.

—St. Pope John Paul II[217]

The phrase "Blessed Sacrament" refers specifically to the Eucharist
"as one of the seven sacraments instituted by Christ to be received
by the faithful. Unlike the other [six] sacraments, however, the Eucharist is not only a sacrament to be received but also a sacrament
to be adored before, during, and after reception. It is therefore a
permanent sacrament, since Christ remains in the Eucharist [truly

---

[217] Homily at Phoenix Park, Dublin, September 29, 1979.

present in His body, blood, soul and divinity] as long as the physical properties [that is, the 'accidents' or 'characteristics'] of the species of bread and wine remain essentially unchanged."[218] The phrase "Blessed Sacrament" is also "A name given to the Holy Eucharist, especially the consecrated elements reserved in the tabernacle [inside a Catholic church or oratory] for adoration, or for the sick."[219]

But what about the phrase "*Most* Blessed Sacrament"? Does this phrase somehow imply that the Eucharist is "the most blessed" of all seven sacraments—and thus it is somehow exalted over the other sacraments of Baptism, Confirmation, Matrimony, Holy Orders, Penance, and the Anointing of the Sick? Yes! Why is this? Because while the other six sacraments *effect* the very grace they signify, the Eucharist *is* what it signifies: it *is* the Body, Blood, Soul and Divinity of our Lord Jesus Christ. In other words, in each of the other six sacraments we receive the grace proper to *that* sacrament; but in the Eucharist, we not only receive the grace proper to it, we *also* receive the very Author of Grace Himself (see "The Presence of Christ and the Real Presence of Christ in the Eucharist").

As the *Catechism* sums up, "The mode of Christ's presence under the Eucharistic species is unique [among all the sacraments].... It raises the Eucharist above all the sacraments as "the perfection of the spiritual life and the end to which all the sacraments tend" (CCC 1374). Indeed, in the most Blessed Sacrament, we have the unique, true presence of Christ in the Eucharist under the appearances of bread and wine, and Holy Mother Church invites the faithful to deepen their faith in the Real Presence of Christ through both adoration and Communion at the Eucharistic liturgy, and through adoration outside the celebration of Mass.

---

[218] MCD, 69.
[219] CCC glossary, s.v. "Blessed Sacrament"; see CCC 1330.

Why We Reserve the Blessed Sacrament

I was sick and you visited me.

—Matthew 25:36

Devotion to the Blessed Sacrament is the queen of all devotions. It is the central devotion of the Church. All others gather round it, and group themselves there as satellites; for others celebrate His mysteries; this is Himself. It is the universal devotion. No one can be without it, in order to be a Christian. How can a man be a Christian who does not worship the living Presence of Christ?

—Fr. Frederick Faber[220]

Throughout the centuries, the Church has taken great care to reserve the most Blessed Sacrament with all due reverence and devotion. As faithful Catholic Christians, we do well to remind ourselves why this is so. After all, why not just consume all of the sacred Hosts that are consecrated at Mass? Why reserve them in the tabernacle?

The Church teaches that "the celebration of the eucharist in the sacrifice of the Mass, is truly the origin and the goal of the worship

[220] Fr. Frederick Faber, *The Blessed Sacrament: The Works and Ways of God* (London: Burns and Oates, 1861), section VII.

which is shown to the eucharist outside Mass."[221] Worship of the
Eucharist outside of the Mass takes two principal forms: first, the
sacred species are reserved after Mass so that the faithful who cannot be present at Mass (above all the sick and those advanced in
age) may receive Holy Communion outside of Mass, for example,
in their home or in a hospital or nursing home when it is taken to
them by a properly deputed extraordinary minister of Holy Communion; second, reservation of the sacred species also permits
the practice of adoration of this great sacrament (see CCC 1379).
Regarding this latter form of worship of the Eucharist outside of
Mass, I am always greatly moved whenever I am at a holy hour of
Eucharistic adoration in which all the lights in the Church are
dimmed with the exception of those focused on the altar on which
the Blessed Sacrament is exposed in a magnificent monstrance,
flanked by candles, and with clouds of rising, fragrant incense.
As Pope St. Paul VI teaches, "The Catholic Church has held firm
to this belief in the presence of Christ's Body and Blood in the
Eucharist not only in her teaching but in her life as well, since she
has at all times paid this great Sacrament the worship known as
'latria,' which may be given to God alone."[222] The *Catechism* states
the following about the Eucharist in our midst:

> It is highly fitting that Christ should have wanted to remain
> present to his Church in this unique way. Since Christ
> was about to take his departure from his own in his visible
> form, he wanted to give us his sacramental presence; since
> he was about to offer himself on the cross to save us, he
> wanted us to have the memorial of the love with which he

---

[221] Congregation of Rites, Instruction *Eucharisticum Mysterium* (May
25, 1967), no. 542.

[222] *Mysterium Fidei* 55.

loved us "to the end," even to the giving of his life. In his Eucharistic presence, he remains mysteriously in our midst as the one who loved us and gave himself up for us, and he remains under signs that express and communicate this love. (CCC 1380)

I remember a particular Eucharistic adoration chapel that I would visit frequently while on assignment. Above the exposed Eucharist in the monstrance, on the wall, was a beautifully scripted sign with a quote attributed to St. Teresa of Calcutta. It read: "The Eucharist is the continuing presence of our Lord's Sacred Incarnation among us." Indeed, He is truly present, in His Body, Blood, Soul, and Divinity in the consecrated hosts reserved in our churches. As Pope St. John Paul II instructs us, "Jesus awaits us in this sacrament of love. Let us not refuse the time to go to meet Him in adoration, in contemplation full of faith, and open to making amends for the serious offenses and crimes of the world. Let our adoration never cease."[223] Indeed, whenever we find ourselves in the presence of the Most Blessed Sacrament, let one of our prayers be this traditional favorite: "O Sacrament Most Holy, O Sacrament Divine, all praise and all thanksgiving be every moment Thine!" Amen.

[223] Pope St. John Paul II, Letter *Dominicae Cenae* (February 24, 1980), no. 3.

Why Do We Fast before Receiving Holy Communion, and What Does Fasting Entail?

And Jesus said to them, "Can the wedding guests mourn as long as the bridegroom is with them? The days will come, when the bridegroom is taken away from them, and then they will fast."

—Matthew 9:15

Fasting (when rightly practiced) lifts the mind to God and mortifies the flesh. It makes virtue easy to attain and increases our merits.

—St. Francis de Sales[224]

The Church has always taught that "refraining from food and drink as an expression of interior penance, in imitation of the fast of Jesus for forty days in the desert"[225] should be a staple element of one's spiritual life, health permitting. Fasting is also "an ascetical practice recommended in Scripture and the writings of the Church Fathers; it is sometimes prescribed by a precept of the Church, especially during the liturgical season of Lent."[226] For example, one

---

[224] Schroeder, *Every Day Is a Gift*, 32.
[225] CCC glossary, s.v. "fasting"; CCC 538, 1434, 2043.
[226] CCC glossary, s.v. "fasting."

of the Church's precepts is that the faithful shall observe the days of fasting and abstinence established by the Church.

When practiced with Christian fervor, fasting—an exercise in self-denial—also sets one apart from the culture at large in a day and age that celebrates instant gratification—from instant messaging, to the fastest of fast food, to the quickest of music downloads from the internet. So, while fasting primarily and usually refers to refraining or abstaining from certain foods, it may also pertain to refraining or abstaining from—or lessening one's use of—non-food products, such as television, sporting events, eating out, and use of the Internet and social media.

In the Latin Rite Church, the Eucharistic fast lasts one hour. The Church is clear on this point: "Whoever is to receive the blessed Eucharist is to abstain for at least one hour before Holy Communion from all food and drink with the sole exception of water and medicine."[227] The same Canon (§3) also states, "the elderly and those who are suffering from some illness, as well as those who care for them, may receive the Blessed Eucharist even if within the preceding hour they have consumed something."[228] But the norm *is* one hour—minimum—before receiving Holy Communion.

One final point: it is not only fasting that is deemed important when preparing to receive our Blessed Lord in Holy Communion. The *Catechism* also states that bodily demeanor—such as gestures and fashion—ought to convey the respect, solemnity, and joy of this moment when Christ becomes our guest" (CCC 1387). Indeed, let us give our best to our Lord, truly present in the most Holy Eucharist.

[227] Canon 919.
[228] Canon 919.

Minister of the Eucharist versus Extraordinary Minister of Holy Communion

Now there are varieties of gifts, but the same Spirit; and there are varieties of service, but the same Lord; and there are varieties of working, but it is the same God who inspires them all in every one.

— 1 Corinthians 12:4-6

In the Church there is a diversity of ministry but a oneness of mission. Christ conferred on the Apostles and their successors the duty of teaching, sanctifying, and ruling in His name and power. But the laity likewise share in the priestly, prophetic, and royal office of Christ and therefore have their own share in the mission of the whole people of God in the Church and in the world.

— Apostolicam Actuositatem 2

What, exactly, is the difference between a "minister of the Eucharist" and an "extraordinary minister of Holy Communion"? The distinction is simple and revolves around the sacrament of Holy Orders.

The Church teaches that "the only minister who can confect the Sacrament of the Eucharist *in persona Christi* [Latin: "in the person of Christ"] is a validly ordained priest."[229] This being so, the title "minister of the Eucharist" belongs properly to the priest alone. Furthermore, by reason of their sacred ordination, *ordinary* ministers of Holy Communion (that is, when it comes to distributing Holy Communion) are the bishop, the priest, *and* the deacon.

Extraordinary ministers of Holy Communion, on the other hand, fall under one of three categories. First, there is the formally instituted acolyte, who, by virtue of his or her office is an extraordinary minister of Holy Communion even outside the celebration of Mass; for example, to take Holy Communion to the sick and home-bound. Second, if real necessity calls for it, a lay member of Christ's faithful may be deputed by the diocesan bishop, pastor, or priest celebrant for the temporary function of extraordinary minister of Holy Communion for one occasion *or* for a specified time. And third, in special cases of an unforeseen nature, permission can also be given to a non-ordained person to distribute Holy Communion for a single occasion by the priest who presides at *that particular* Eucharistic celebration.

Distribution of Holy Communion by a layperson is to be understood strictly according to the name by which it is known: that of "extraordinary minister of Holy Communion" and *not* "extraordinary minister of the Eucharist." This distinction helps us to avoid confusion between ordained and non-ordained ministerial functions.

---

[229] Congregation for Divine Worship and the Discipline of the Sacraments, Instruction *Redemptionis Sacramentum* (March 25, 2004), 154, referencing *Code of Canon Law*, 900§1.

Eucharistic Miracles

*Then he ordered the crowds to sit down on the grass; and taking the
five loaves and the two fish he looked up to heaven, and blessed, and
broke and gave the loaves to the disciples, and the disciples gave them
to the crowds. And they all ate and were satisfied. And they took up
twelve baskets full of the broken pieces left over. And those who ate
were about five thousand men, besides women and children.*

—Matthew 14:19-21

*He [Christ] declared that the chalice, which comes from his creation,
was his blood, and he makes it the nourishment of our blood. He
affirmed that the bread, which comes from his creation, was his body,
and he makes it the nourishment of our body. When the chalice we mix
and the bread we bake receive the word of God, the eucharistic elements
become the body and blood of Christ, by which our bodies live and grow.*

—St. Irenaeus[230]

The Catholic Church teaches that the Eucharist is "the source
and summit of the Christian life."[231] This is because "The other

---

[230] From the treatise *Against Heresies*, Lib. 5, 2, 2-3: SC 153, 30-38,
    in *Liturgy of the Hours*, vol. II, 727-728.
[231] *Lumen Gentium* 11; CCC 1324.

sacraments, as well as with every ministry of the Church and every work of the apostolate, are tied together with the Eucharist and are directed toward it. The most Blessed Eucharist contains the entire spiritual boon of the Church, that is, Christ himself."[232]

As Catholics, we believe that Jesus Christ is truly, really, and substantially present in the most Holy Eucharist. From the words of Consecration onwards at Mass, the elements of bread and wine are no longer bread and wine, but rather—through the miracle of transubstantiation—are changed into the very substance of our Lord's Body and Blood. While the "accidents" or outward "characteristics" of bread and wine remain after the words of Consecration, our faith tells us that Our Lord is truly present in the Eucharist. Notice, too, that St. Paul teaches that *"Faith comes from what is heard"* (Rom. 10:17), and we indeed *hear* the words of Consecration at Mass.

Over the centuries, numerous Eucharistic miracles have taken place in which the reserved Eucharistic Host has taken on the outward characteristics — the physicality and visual appearance — of human flesh and blood. For example, Italy, Poland, Germany, France, Belgium, Austria, Portugal, the Netherlands, Spain, and Switzerland are just some of the countries where Eucharistic miracles have taken place that the Church has deemed worthy of belief. The Eucharistic miracles of Lanciano, Italy, during the eighth century and that of Santarem in Portugal in 1247 are just two of the many examples where critical studies and scientific analyses have played a role in validating the miraculous occurrence of a consecrated wheaten Host having turned into human flesh and blood. In some cases, scientific and medical experts have been

---

[232] Second Vatican Council, Decree on the Ministry and Life of Priests *Presbyterorum Ordinis* (December 7, 1965), no. 5.

able to determine that the human flesh is in fact human heart tissue—bringing to mind our Lord's own Sacred Heart, a part of His sacred humanity as the God-Man.

While belief in these miracles is not required of the faithful, such supernatural occurrences can help increase our faith in our Eucharistic doctrine. In fact, many of these miracles took place precisely at a moment when someone doubted our Lord's Real Presence in the Eucharist. What a gift we have in this "source and summit of the Christian life"! As the saying goes that is familiar among Catholics: "The Real Presence is a Real Present."

Confession and the Gift of God's Mercy

"Father, I have sinned against heaven and before you; I am no longer worthy to be called your son; treat me as one of your hired servants." And he arose and came to his father. But while he was yet at a distance, his father saw him and had compassion, and ran and embraced him and kissed him.

—Luke 15:18–20

Do not despair of his mercy, no matter how great your sins, for great mercy will take away great sins.

For the Lord is gracious and merciful and prefers the conversion of a sinner rather than his death.

—St. Jerome[233]

What, exactly, do the Sacrament of Penance and God's mercy have in common? Our Lord Himself gives us a beautiful answer to this question in something He told St. Faustina Kowalska, the Divine Mercy seer:

> Write, speak of My mercy. Tell souls where they are to look for solace; that is, in the Tribunal of Mercy [the Sacrament

---

[233] *Commentary on the Book of Joel*, PL 25, 967–968, in *Liturgy of the Hours*, vol. IV, 178.

of Reconciliation]. There the greatest miracles take place [and] are incessantly repeated. To avail oneself of this miracle … it suffices to come with faith to the feet of My representative and to reveal to him one's misery, and the miracle of Divine Mercy will be fully demonstrated. Were a soul like a decaying corpse so that from a human standpoint, there would be no [hope of] restoration and everything would already be lost, it is not so with God. The miracle of Divine Mercy restores that soul in full. Oh, how miserable are those who do not take advantage of the miracle of God's mercy![234]

This passage should provide each one of us with great comfort and hope. In the Sacrament of Confession, our Blessed Lord is ever ready to welcome back the truly repentant sinner—the prodigal son or daughter. This sacrament is where we take our mortal sins to be reconciled with God, and are welcome to take our venial sins as well. In fact, for those who partake of the Sacrament of Confession faithfully and regularly—for example, once a month, say, in honor of the First Friday devotion to the Sacred Heart of Jesus or on the First Saturday of each month in honor of the Immaculate Heart of Mary—hopefully it will *only* be venial sins that will need to be confessed, as the person will have habitually grown in virtue to shun every mortal sin precisely through the practice of regular, monthly Confession.

Regarding those persons who may be fearful of Confession—for example, out of fear or shame—our Lord relayed to St. Faustina these comforting words: "Pray for souls that they be not afraid to approach the tribunal of My mercy. Do not grow weary of praying for sinners. You know what a burden their souls are to My Heart. Relieve my deathly sorrow; dispense My mercy."[235]

[234] *Diary* 1448.
[235] *Diary* 975.

Benefits of a Frequent Confession

"I desire mercy, and not sacrifice."

—Matthew 12:7

Write, speak of My mercy. Tell souls where they are to look for solace;
that is, in the Tribunal of Mercy [the Sacrament of Reconciliation].
There the greatest miracles take place [and] are incessantly repeated.

—Words of Our Lord Jesus Christ to St. Faustina[236]

Although it is true that the Church's canon law requires that we
confess our sins at least once a year (again, this is one of the precepts
of the Church; see "The Precepts of the Church"), even more to
be desired is the Church's time-honored tradition of confessing
one's sins at least once a month. Whether confessing mortal or
venial sins, the benefits to be gained from a frequent Confession
are many. For example, apart from the obvious effect of being
forgiven of one's sins, frequent Confession brings with it a purify-
ing of conscience; in the soul, grace is increased; the human will
is strengthened to do better in daily life and yearns to advance in
virtue; self-knowledge is increased to know one's strengths and

---

[236] *Diary* 1448.

weaknesses better; more rapid growth in virtue takes place overall; the virtue of humility grows; assistance is given to overcome bad habits and any spirit of mediocrity in the spiritual life; and greater self-control is achieved in daily living. Frequent Confession also helps us to advance in the spiritual life and to be more faithful to our daily duty, regardless of our vocation—whether single or married; widowed; a consecrated bishop, priest, or deacon; or a vowed contemplative or active religious.

Both Pope Pius XII and Pope St. Paul VI provide a synthesis on this important teaching. Pope Pius XII defended the practice of frequent Confession, for example, even of venial sins. "By it," he said, "self-knowledge is increased, Christian humility grows, bad habits are corrected, spiritual neglect and tepidity are resisted, the conscience is purified, the will is strengthened, a salutary self-control is attained, and grace is increased in virtue of the sacrament itself."[237] And Pope St. Paul VI, in promulgating the new rite of the Sacrament of Penance following Vatican II, stressed what he called the "great value" of "frequent and reverent recourse to this Sacrament (of Confession) even when only venial sins are in question." In the same promulgation, he also stated that such a practice "is a constant effort to bring to perfection the grace of our Baptism."[238] Pope St. John Paul II sums up these multiple benefits of Confession with this point of wisdom concerning one's vocation: "It would be an illusion to seek after holiness, according to the vocation one has received from God, without partaking frequently of this sacrament of conversion and reconciliation. Those who go to

---

[237] Pope Pius XII, Encyclical *Mystici Corporis Christi* (June 29, 1943), no. 88.

[238] Accompanying the promulgation of the *Ordo Paenitentiae* (December 2, 1973).

Confession frequently, and do so with the desire to make progress, will notice the strides that they make in their spiritual lives."[239]

It's important to remember, too, that just as unchecked everyday faults and weaknesses can lead one to commit venial sin, so unchecked venial sins can lead one to commit mortal sin. St. Augustine, in his first homily on the Epistle of St. John, makes clear this truth when he says, "While he is in the flesh, man cannot help but have at least some light sins.... if you take them for light when you weigh them, tremble when you count them. A number of light objects makes a great mass; a number of drops fills a river; a number of grains makes a heap. What then is our hope? Above all, confession"[240] (CCC 1863).

---

[239] Pope St. John Paul II, Address to participants at a conference of the Apostolic Penitentiary, Rome, March 27, 2004.
[240] *In ep. Jo.* 1, 6: *PL* 35, 1982.

Marriage as between One Man and One Woman

Therefore a man leaves his father and his mother and cleaves to his wife, and they become one flesh.

—Genesis 2:24

Those who marry should be united with the bishop's approval, so that the marriage may follow God's will and not merely the prompting of the flesh. Let everything be done for God's honor.

—St. Ignatius of Antioch[241]

One of the Catholic Church's most succinct and unchanging moral and dogmatic teachings is that marriage is meant to be solely between one man and one woman for life. As instituted by Almighty God, "the matrimonial covenant, by which a man and a woman establish between themselves a partnership of the whole of life, is by its nature ordered toward the good of the spouses and the procreation and education of offspring; this covenant between baptized persons has been raised by Christ the Lord to the dignity of a sacrament" (CCC 1601).

---

[241] From a *Letter to Polycarp*, 5, 1–8, 1. 3: Funk 1, 249–253, in *Liturgy of the Hours*, vol. III, 568.

As noted in the *Catechism*, "The vocation to marriage is written in the very nature of man and woman as they came from the hand of the Creator" (CCC 1603). So it is, then, that marriage is said to be an important part of the natural law and "not a purely human institution" (CCC 1603). Marriage by its very nature is meant to be exclusive, faithful, unitive, fruitful, and procreative—embracing fully the gift of children according to God's most holy will. This is meant to be beneficial not only for the spouses and the children themselves, but for the stability and benefit of society at large.

The Church teaches very clearly that, "Sacred Scripture *begins* with the creation of man and woman in the image and likeness of God and *concludes* with a vision of 'the wedding-feast of the Lamb'" (CCC 1602, emphasis added). We can say, therefore, that "man and woman" and "marriage" are literally the two "bookends" of the entire Bible—indeed, of the entire story of salvation history. And let us not forget, too, that the *first* public miracle performed by Christ was conducted at a wedding feast in Cana of Galilee (see John 2:1-11).

Man and woman are equal in their dignity, yet different in their specific gender characteristics and gifts. Each one benefits from these natural gifts of the other. We can say that, as created beings, man and woman are different from, but *made for*, each other:

> Holy Scripture affirms that man and woman were created for one another: "It is not good that the man should be alone." The woman, "flesh of his flesh," his equal, his nearest in all things, is given to him by God as a "helpmate"; she thus represents God from whom comes our help. "Therefore a man leaves his father and his mother and cleaves to his wife, and they become one flesh." The Lord himself shows that this signifies an unbreakable union of their two lives by recalling what the plan of the Creator had

been "in the beginning": "So they are no longer two, but one flesh." (CCC 1605)

Because God instituted its seminal framework at the time of creation, marriage between one man and one woman is a most fundamental human and social institution tied to the reality of the natural law; and "though it is regulated by civil laws and church laws, it did not originate from either the church or state, but from God. Therefore, neither church nor state can alter the basic meaning and structure of marriage."[242] Indeed, "from the beginning" (see Matt. 19:8-9), marriage between one man and one woman for life has been an intimate part of God's plan for His creation, a plan that regards greatly and takes into account the dignity of the human person made in His image and likeness and His plan, as well, for the propagation of the human race and the great gift of human life. Indeed, "marriage makes a unique and irreplaceable contribution to the common good of society, especially through the procreation and education of children. The union of husband and wife becomes, over a lifetime, a great good for themselves, their family, communities, and society. Marriage is a gift to be cherished and protected."[243] As baptized, faithful Christians, let us always do our part to defend valiantly the Sacrament—and sacred institution—of Matrimony, a sacrament that mirrors and images the relationship between Our Lord Jesus Christ and His Bride, the Church.

---

[242] USCCB, "Between Man and Woman: Questions and Answers about Marriage and Same-Sex Unions," United States Conference of Catholic Bishops, https://www.usccb.org/topics/promotion -defense-marriage/between-man-and-woman-questions-and -answers-about-marriage-and.

[243] USCCB, "Between Man and Woman."

Liturgy

Use of Latin in the Sacred Liturgy

Many of the Jews read this title, for the place where Jesus was crucified was near the city; and it was written in Hebrew, in Latin, and in Greek.

—John 19:20

The sacred liturgy is above all things the worship of the divine Majesty.

—Vatican II's Constitution on the Sacred Liturgy, *Sacrosanctum Concilium*, no. 33

The Latin Rite Church,[244] both during and after Vatican II, has continued to encourage the use of Latin during the celebration of

---

[244] In the Catholic Church, the Latin (or Roman) Rite, is found in two primary forms: the *Ordinary Form* (i.e., the Reformed Roman Rite of the Second Vatican Council) and the *Extraordinary Form* (i.e., the Tridentine/Traditional Latin Mass), the latter made possible by concession of the Holy See (see *Traditionis Custodes*, Apostolic Letter issued "Motu Proprio" by Pope Francis, July 16, 2021). By concession of the Holy See, their also exists within the Latin Rite the Anglican Use Liturgy. Also, there are twenty-three Eastern Rites of the Catholic Church, such as the Armenian,

Mass. Nevertheless, the Church's teaching on this topic has never really seemed to flourish since 1963, the year that *Sacrosanctum Concilium*, the Constitution on the Sacred Liturgy, was promulgated by the council.

While it is true that Vatican II encouraged that the vernacular—the ordinary, native languages of different countries—be employed in the liturgy so as to encourage a greater participation on the part of the faithful gathered together for sacred worship, it was never intended that the Church's own *universal* "mother tongue"—Latin—should be done away with altogether. In fact, *Sacrosanctum Concilium* says, "the Latin language is to be preserved in the Latin rites" of the Church, and "steps should be taken so that the faithful may also be able to say or to sing together in Latin those parts of the Ordinary of the Mass which pertain to them."[245] Examples of the "Ordinary" parts of the Mass would include the Gloria (the Glory to God in the Highest), the Credo (the Nicene-Constantinopolitan Creed), the Sanctus (the Holy, Holy, Holy), the Pater Noster (the Our Father), and the Angus Dei (the Lamb of God).

Another important point regarding the use of Latin and sacred music: *Sacrosanctum Concilium* also states, "the Church acknowledges Gregorian chant as specially suited to the Roman liturgy," and that as such, "it should be given pride of place in liturgical services."[246] As faithful Catholics, then, who want to be faithful to the teachings of Vatican II, we should all do our part—such as encouraging the pastors of the Church—to promote and encourage the use of Latin in the celebration of the Sacred Liturgy.

Byzantine, Chaldean, and Coptic Rites, all fully Catholic and in union with the Roman Church, under the pope.

[245] *Sacrosanctum Concilium* 36, 54.
[246] *Sacrosanctum Concilium* 116.

Sacrificial Nature of the Mass — Not Just a Meal

For as often as you eat this bread and drink the cup, you proclaim the Lord's death until he comes.

— 1 Corinthians 11:26

When you look at the crucifix, you understand how much Jesus loved you. When you look at the Sacred Host, you understand how much Jesus loves you now.

— St. Teresa of Calcutta[247]

According to Catholic sacramental theology, the Mass should be seen as both a sacrifice *and* a meal — that is, as a *sacred* banquet. Unfortunately, however, in modern times, it often seems that the sacrificial nature of the Mass is either lost sight of, ignored, or at least downplayed. As committed Catholics, we have a duty to both possess and help foster a *balanced view* of the reality of the Mass as *both* sacrifice *and* banquet — and the best of banquets at

---

[247] Fr. Martin Lucia, SS.CC., *Rosary Meditations from Mother Teresa of Calcutta: Loving Jesus with the Heart of Mary, Eucharistic Meditations on the Fifteen Mysteries of the Rosary* (N.p.: Missionaries of Charity, 1984), 1.

that, to use imagery from the book of Revelation regarding all of the saved being seated at the Marriage Supper of the Lamb (see Rev. 19:7-9).

Holy Mass re-presents—that is, it "makes present again"—the *one* sacrificial act of our Lord Jesus Christ, the Lamb of God: His having died on the Cross to redeem and save us. In his 1965 encyclical *Mysterium Fidei*, Pope St. Paul VI writes, "By means of the Mystery of the Eucharist, the Sacrifice of the Cross which was *once* carried out on Calvary is *re-enacted* in wonderful fashion and is constantly recalled, and its salvific power is applied to the forgiving of the sins we commit each day."[248]

Despite the claims of some non-Catholics to the contrary, the Catholic Church does *not* teach that the holy Mass, although celebrated daily and throughout the world, constitutes a crucifixion of our Blessed Lord "over and over again." Indeed, this would be a heresy. Rather, holy Mass makes present again the *one saving action* of our Lord on Calvary. The *Catechism* sums this up nicely when it states, "The redemptive sacrifice of Christ is unique, accomplished *once* for all; yet it is made present in the Eucharistic sacrifice of the Church. The same is true of the one priesthood of Christ; it is made present through the ministerial priesthood without diminishing the uniqueness of Christ's priesthood: 'Only Christ is the true priest, the others being only his ministers'" (CCC 1545, referencing St. Thomas Aquinas, emphasis added).

Thus, it is worth reiterating what was stated in "The Lamb as an Emblem of Docility": "The perfect sacrifice was Christ's death

---

[248] Pope St. Paul VI, Encyclical Letter *Mysterium Fidei* (September 3, 1965), no. 27, emphasis added.

on the cross; by this sacrifice, Christ accomplished our redemption as high priest of the new and eternal covenant. The sacrifice of Christ on the cross is commemorated and mysteriously made present in the Eucharistic sacrifice of the Church."[249]

---

[249] CCC glossary, s.v. "sacrifice"; see CCC 616, 1357, 1544, 1545, 2099.

Universal Prayer of the Mass

And they devoted themselves to the apostles' teaching and fellowship, to the breaking of bread and the prayers.

—Acts 2:42

The person who thinks only of himself says only prayers of petition; the one who thinks of his neighbor says prayers of intercession; whoever thinks only of loving and serving God says prayers of abandonment to God's will, and this is the prayer of the saints.

—Ven. Fulton J. Sheen[250]

The Universal Prayer—also known as the Prayer of the Faithful, Bidding Prayers, or General Intercessions—is that part of the Mass that immediately follows the praying of the Nicene-Constantinopolitan Creed at the Sunday liturgy, or which may follow the Gospel or homily at a weekday liturgy. The Universal Prayer is normally to be included whenever there are people attending the Mass. In it, "the people exercise their priestly function by praying for all

---

[250] "Quotes from Bishop Sheen," Archbishop Fulton John Sheen Spiritual Centre, http://www.archbishopfultonsheencentre.com/Quotes.html.

mankind."²⁵¹ According to *The General Instruction of the Roman Missal* (GIRM) the series of intentions for the Universal Prayer is usually to be: "For the needs of the Church; for public authorities and the salvation of the whole world; for those burdened by any kind of difficulty; [and] for the local community."²⁵² During Masses for special occasions, these categories of intentions for the Universal Prayer may be adjusted accordingly. The priest-celebrant begins the Universal Prayer with an invitation to offer the particular intentions, and he concludes them as well. A deacon or a lay person (such as an instituted lector) may read each intention, while the congregation gives an appropriate response after each one, such as, "Lord, hear our prayer."

So it is that the Universal Prayer enables worshipers gathered at holy Mass to pray for all mankind by exercising their common "priesthood of the faithful" — not to be confused with the ministerial priesthood received through the Sacrament of Holy Orders (see "Priestly Ordination Reserved to Men Alone"). This is what we mean by the phrase, "the priestly people of God." Christ has made of His Church a "kingdom of priests" (see Rev. 1:6), and He gives the faithful a share in His priesthood through the Sacraments of Baptism and Confirmation. The *Catechism* teaches that the faithful participate in "Christ's mission as priest, prophet, and king" when they exercise their common priesthood, "each according to his own vocation" (see CCC 1546), and the Universal Prayer of the Mass shows forth this wonderful fact. As noted so beautifully in the GIRM, "In the Universal Prayer or Prayer of the Faithful,

---

²⁵¹ MCD, 431.

²⁵² USCCB, *General Instruction of the Roman Missal* [GIRM], USCCB Liturgy Documentary Series 14 (Washington, D.C.: United States Conference of Catholic Bishops, 2010), p. 30, Item 70.

the people respond in some sense to the Word of God which they have received in faith and, exercising the office of their baptismal Priesthood, offer prayers to God for the salvation of all."[253] Indeed, as a *priestly people*, then, we are also an *intercessory people*, praying to God on behalf of all of our brothers and sisters.

[253] *GIRM*, Item 69.

Proper Placement of the Tabernacle

And the Word became flesh and dwelt among us, full of grace and truth; we have beheld his glory, glory as of the only Son from the Father.

—John 1:14

The tabernacle is to be situated "in churches in a most worthy place with the greatest honor." The dignity, placing, and security of the Eucharistic tabernacle should foster adoration before the Lord really present in the Blessed Sacrament of the altar.

—CCC 1183[254]

The word *tabernacle* means dwelling place. The Latin word *tabernaculum* is a bit more specific: it means *tent*—and, of course, a tent is a dwelling place. Through His Sacred Incarnation and through His Real and abiding Presence in the Eucharist, our Lord Jesus Christ has "pitched His tent among us." Think, here, of the *Angelus* prayer, when at the end of that prayer the versicle and response are said: V. "And the Word became flesh", R. "And

---

[254] Quoting Pope St. Paul VI, *Mysterium Fidei*: AAS (1965): 771; cf. *Sacrosanctum Concilium* 128.

dwelt among us." Well, we can also say that the Word became flesh and has *"pitched His tent among us"* (and mean it!) because that's exactly what every tabernacle in a Catholic church is doing: providing a dwelling place for our Lord Jesus Christ truly present in the most Holy Eucharist.

In Catholic churches throughout the world, the Blessed Sacrament is reserved in the tabernacle primarily to take the Eucharist to those who are not able to be present at Mass, above all the sick and those advanced in age (see CCC 1379 and "Why We Reserve the Blessed Sacrament"). In addition, "this reservation also permits the practice of adoring this great Sacrament and offering it the worship due to God. Accordingly, forms of adoration that are not only private but also public and communitarian in nature, as established or approved by the Church herself, must be greatly promoted."[255] Because of the practice of Eucharistic adoration, the proper placement of the tabernacle within the church building is crucial because its prominence illustrates precisely what we Catholics believe about the Eucharist: that it is the real, true, and abiding Presence of our Lord Jesus Christ.

Nevertheless, the proper placement of the tabernacle has been a topic of some confusion over the years, despite the fact that the Church's teaching on the subject is quite clear. For example, Pope Benedict XVI provides a nice summation of all that the Church has said on this subject since Vatican II:

> In churches which do not have a Blessed Sacrament *chapel*, and where the high altar with its tabernacle is still in place, it is appropriate to continue to use this structure for the reservation and adoration of the Eucharist, taking care not

---

[255] *Redemptionis Sacramentum* 129.

to place the celebrant's chair in front of it. In new churches, it is good to position the Blessed Sacrament chapel close to the sanctuary; where this is not possible, it is preferable to locate the tabernacle in the sanctuary, in a sufficiently *elevated place*, at the center of the apse area, or in another place where it will be equally conspicuous. Attention to these considerations will lend dignity to the tabernacle, which must always be cared for.[256]

For faithful Catholics, the main point to remember is that the prominent, unobstructed "correct positioning of the tabernacle contributes to the recognition of Christ's Real Presence in the Blessed Sacrament. Therefore, the place where the Eucharistic species are reserved, marked by a sanctuary lamp, should be readily visible to everyone entering the church"[257] and not in some obscure location. And the sanctuary lamp—with a *real* "living flame" signifying our Lord's *Real* Presence—should clearly mark it.

---

[256] Pope Benedict XVI, Post-synodal Apostolic Exhortation *Sacramentum Caritatis* (February 22, 2007), no. 69, emphasis added.
[257] *Sacramentum Caritatis* 69.

What Is Eucharistic Adoration?

Jesus then said to them, "Truly, truly, I say to you, it was not Moses who gave you the bread from heaven; my Father gives you the true bread from heaven. For the bread of God is that which comes down from heaven, and gives life to the world."

—John 6:32–33

The Eucharist is "the source and summit of the Christian life." "The other sacraments, and indeed all ecclesiastical ministries and works of the apostolate, are bound up with the Eucharist and are oriented toward it. For in the blessed Eucharist is contained the whole spiritual good of the Church, namely Christ himself, our Pasch."

—CCC 1324[258]

As taught by Vatican II, the Eucharist is "the source and summit of the Christian life."[259] In the celebration of the Eucharist, when the priest says the words of Consecration at Mass, the bread and wine are changed into the Body and Blood of Christ—a miraculous change, which the Catholic Church calls *transubstantiation*. As a

---

[258] Quoting *Lumen Gentium* 11 and *Presbyterorum Ordinis* 5.
[259] *Lumen Gentium* 11; CCC 1324.

result, the whole Christ, Body, Blood, Soul, and Divinity is really, truly, and substantially present, under either Eucharistic species, in both the consecrated bread and the consecrated wine. And while we can both adore and receive our Lord in Holy Communion at Mass, we can also adore Him outside of Mass in His true and abiding Real Presence in what is referred to as "Eucharistic adoration."

With Eucharistic adoration, the Eucharist is exposed in a monstrance—a vessel made of precious metal that holds a large, consecrated Host behind glass so that it may be gazed upon by adorers of this most Blessed Sacrament. This is done at set times during the week established by the pastor of a parish and includes adorers who sign up for a committed hour. But Eucharistic adoration may also include *perpetual* adoration that is ongoing in a chapel constructed just for that purpose—24 hours a day, 7 days a week.

We can also adore our Lord in His sacramental Presence by simply praying before a tabernacle wherein the Blessed Sacrament is reserved, for example, inside a church, chapel, or oratory. The tabernacle was originally intended for the reservation of the Eucharist in a "worthy place" so that it could be brought to those absent from Mass—for example, the sick and those advanced in age (see CCC 1379 and "Why We Reserve the Blessed Sacrament"). But "as faith in the real presence of Christ in the Eucharist deepened, the Church became conscious of the meaning of silent adoration of the Lord truly present under the Eucharistic species" (CCC 1379). The benefit of this truth is that one can partake of Eucharistic adoration even if the Blessed Sacrament is *not* exposed in a monstrance in an adoration chapel. Again, one can do this by simply visiting a Catholic church and taking time to pray before the tabernacle.

Worship and Veneration

Holy, holy, holy is the LORD of hosts;
the whole earth is full of his glory.

—Isaiah 6:3

The Catholic Church has held firm to this belief in the presence of
Christ's Body and Blood in the Eucharist not only in her teaching but
in her life as well, since she has at all times paid this great Sacrament
the worship known as "latria," which may be given to God alone. As St.
Augustine says: "It was in His flesh that Christ walked among us and it
is His flesh that He has given us to eat for our salvation; but no one eats
of this flesh without having first adored it … and not only do we not sin
in thus adoring it, but we would be sinning if we did not do so."

—Pope St. Paul VI[260]

Strictly speaking, "worship" is properly given to Almighty God alone—to the three divine Persons of the Most Holy Trinity: Father, Son, and Holy Spirit. "Veneration," on the other hand, is given to the saints and to the angels while "the greatest of veneration" is given to the Blessed Virgin Mary alone.

---

[260] *Mysterium Fidei* 55.

Sacred Tradition gives us three words to help make these important distinctions between worship and veneration: *latria* is a Greek-rooted Latin term that refers to "worship" *per se*, which is to be given to God alone. *Dulia* is another Greek-rooted Latin term that denotes the *kind* and *degree* of "veneration" given to the angels and saints. Lastly, *hyperdulia*—as it sounds—is the greatest form of *dulia* and is reserved for the Blessed Virgin Mary alone because of her unique place among creatures in salvation history. So, *hyperdulia* simply means the "greatest of veneration." Although our Blessed Mother ranks the greatest, then, among all the saints and angels that receive *dulia*, the *hyperdulia* accorded to her is entirely different from the *latria* (worship) reserved for God alone. Worth noting, too, is that some theologians have posited the phrase *protodulia* in reference to St. Joseph. As it means, St. Joseph—as the Guardian of the Redeemer—receives the "first of veneration" among the saints and angels who receive *dulia*.

So, accusations commonly lodged against Catholics of "worshipping" Mary or the saints or angels are simply not true. Catholics worship Almighty God *alone*. But we venerate the angels and saints, in whom God is glorified; and the *greatest* form of veneration is reserved for the holy Mother of God.

One final note: the most Blessed Sacrament receives *latria* because it *is* the Body, Blood, Soul, and Divinity of our Lord Jesus Christ. This is why Eucharistic adoration is so important in the spiritual life.

Blessing—What It Is and from Whom It Comes

The Lord bless you and keep you: the Lord make his face to shine upon you, and be gracious to you: the Lord lift up his countenance upon you, and give you peace.

—Numbers 6:24-26

God is more anxious to bestow His blessings on us than we are to receive them.

—St. Augustine[261]

As discovered in Sacred Scripture, "blessing" can mean several important things: "praise, the desire that good fortune go with a person or thing, dedication of a person or thing to God's service and a gift. In liturgical language a blessing is a ritual ceremony by which an authorized cleric in major orders sanctifies persons or things to divine service, or invokes divine favor on what he blesses. The Church's ritual provides for over two hundred such blessings, some of which are reserved to bishops or members of certain religious institutes."[262] There are also some blessings that can be

---

[261] Thigpen, *A Dictionary of Quotes from the Saints*, 23.
[262] MCD, 69-70.

imparted by members of the lay faithful (e.g., blessing before and after meals, blessing by parents over their children, etc.).

Similarly, the *Catechism* teaches us that "A blessing or benediction is a prayer invoking God's power and care upon some person, place, thing, or undertaking. The prayer of benediction acknowledges God as the source of all blessing. Some blessings confer a permanent status: consecration of persons to God, or setting things apart for liturgical usage,"[263] like sacred vessels or priestly vestments used for the celebration of Holy Mass.

Among the Church's treasury of sacramentals, "*blessings* (of persons, meals, objects and places) come first. Every blessing praises God and prays for his gifts. In Christ, Christians are blessed by God the Father 'with every spiritual blessing' [Eph. 1:3]. This is why the Church imparts blessings by invoking the name of Jesus, usually while making the holy sign of the cross of Christ" (CCC 1671). Thus, blessings are so important in daily life! They *sanctify the present moment* involving persons, places, and things and various situations and circumstances (such as having your parish priest bless your new car), all the while having a lasting effect. So it is, then, that blessings should be abundant in our lives.

[263] CCC glossary, s.v. "blessing"; see CCC 1671, 2626.

The Church's *Book of Blessings*

Blessed be the God and Father of our Lord Jesus Christ, who has blessed us in Christ with every spiritual blessing in the heavenly places.

—Ephesians 1:3

The celebration of blessings holds a privileged place among all the sacramentals created by the Church for the pastoral benefit of the people of God. As a liturgical action, the celebration leads the faithful to praise God and prepares them for the principal effect of the sacraments. By celebrating a blessing the faithful can also sanctify various situations and events in their lives.

—From a Decree from the Congregation for Divine Worship[264]

What an absolute wonderful treasury and gift the Church has in her *Book of Blessings* from the Roman Ritual—a compilation of more than two hundred blessings. The blessings pertain to persons, buildings, and various forms of human activity; to objects designed for use in the liturgy or popular devotions and religious articles that foster the devotion of the Christian people; to objects related

---

[264] Promulgating the Roman Ritual, *Book of Blessings* (New York: Catholic Book Publishing, 1989), 19.

to feasts and seasons and to other needs and occasions, such as the blessing for the welcoming of new parishioners.

Celebrations of blessings hold a privileged place within the life of Holy Mother Church because they can be used in so many pastoral situations. As liturgical actions, celebrations of blessings lead the faithful to praise God and prepare them for the principal effects of the sacraments they receive. By celebrating blessings, the faithful can also sanctify many different situations and events in their lives.

In the Roman Ritual *Book of Blessings*, for example, there is a blessing for sons, daughters, engaged couples, married couples, and couples on their wedding anniversary. There is a blessing for a mother before childbirth and after childbirth, for parents after a miscarriage, and for adoptive parents and their child. There is a blessing for persons suffering from an addiction or substance abuse, and for a victim of crime or oppression. There is a blessing for a new home, school, university, library, hospital, office, shop, or factory. There is a blessing for animals, fields and flocks, tools, boats, fishing gear, and various means of transportation. The list goes on and on! What a gift our Catholic faith is!

A blessing is "an encounter between God and man. In blessing, God's gift and man's acceptance of it are united in dialogue with each other. The prayer of blessing is man's response to God's gifts: because God blesses, the human heart can in return praise the One who is the source of every blessing" (CCC 2626). So let us make good and frequent use of the Church's many blessings upon persons, objects, places, and life's many and various situations—and may these blessings help to sanctify our very lives.

Appendix: Selected Prayers

Daily Prayers

Act of Faith

O my God, I firmly believe that You are one God in three Divine Persons, Father, Son, and Holy Spirit. And I believe that Your Divine Son, Jesus, became man and died for our sins, and that He will come again to judge the living and the dead. I believe these and all the truths that the holy Catholic Church teaches, because You have revealed them, O God, Who can neither deceive nor be deceived. Amen.

Act of Hope

O my God, relying on Your almighty power and infinite mercy and promises, I hope to obtain pardon of my sins, the help of Your grace, and life everlasting, through the merits of Jesus Christ, my Lord and Redeemer. Amen.

Act of Charity

O my God, I love You above all things, with my whole heart and soul, because You are all good and deserving of all my love. I love my neighbor as myself for the love of You. I forgive all those who have injured me, and I ask pardon of all those whom I have injured. Amen.

Act of Contrition

O my God, I am heartily sorry for having offended You, and I detest all my sins because I dread the loss of Heaven and the pains of Hell; but most of all, because they have offended You, my God, Who are all good and deserving of all my love. I firmly resolve, with the help of Your grace, to confess my sins, to do penance, and to amend my life. Amen.

Memorare

Remember, O most gracious Virgin Mary, that never was it known that anyone who fled to thy protection, implored thy help, or sought thine intercession was left unaided. Inspired by this confidence, I fly unto thee, O Virgin of virgins, my mother; to thee do I come, before thee I stand, sinful and sorrowful. O Mother of the Word Incarnate, despise not my petitions, but in thy mercy hear and answer me. Amen.

Sub Tuum Praesidium

We fly to thy protection, O Holy Mother of God, despise not our petitions in our necessities, but deliver us always from all dangers, O glorious and blessed Virgin.

Litany of the Sacred Heart of Jesus

V. Lord, have mercy.
R. Lord, have mercy.

V. Christ, have mercy.

R. Christ, have mercy.

V. Lord, have mercy.

R. Lord, have mercy.

V. Christ, hear us.

R. Christ, hear us.

V. Christ, graciously hear us.

R. Christ, graciously hear us.

God the Father of Heaven,
have mercy on us.

God the Son, Redeemer of the world,
have mercy on us.

God, the Holy Spirit,
have mercy on us.

Holy Trinity, One God,
have mercy on us.

Heart of Jesus, Son of the Eternal Father,
have mercy on us.

Heart of Jesus, formed by the Holy Spirit in the womb
of the Virgin Mother, *have mercy on us.*

Heart of Jesus, substantially united to the Word of God,
have mercy on us.

Heart of Jesus, of Infinite Majesty,
have mercy on us.

Heart of Jesus, Sacred Temple of God,
have mercy on us.

Heart of Jesus, Tabernacle of the Most High,
have mercy on us.

Heart of Jesus, House of God and Gate of Heaven,
have mercy on us.

Heart of Jesus, burning furnace of charity,
have mercy on us.

Heart of Jesus, abode of justice and love,
have mercy on us.

Heart of Jesus, full of goodness and love,
have mercy on us.

Heart of Jesus, abyss of all virtues,
have mercy on us.

Heart of Jesus, most worthy of all praise,
have mercy on us.

Heart of Jesus, King and center of all hearts,
have mercy on us.

Heart of Jesus, in Whom are all treasures of wisdom
and knowledge, *have mercy on us.*

Heart of Jesus, in Whom dwells the fullness of divinity,
have mercy on us.

Heart of Jesus, in Whom the Father was well pleased,
have mercy on us.

Heart of Jesus, of Whose fullness we have all received,
have mercy on us.

Heart of Jesus, desire of the everlasting hills,
have mercy on us.

Heart of Jesus, patient and most merciful,
have mercy on us.

Heart of Jesus, enriching all who invoke Thee,
have mercy on us.

Heart of Jesus, fountain of life and holiness,
have mercy on us.

Heart of Jesus, propitiation for our sins,
have mercy on us.

Heart of Jesus, loaded down with opprobrium,
   have mercy on us.
Heart of Jesus, bruised for our offenses,
   have mercy on us.
Heart of Jesus, obedient to death,
   have mercy on us.
Heart of Jesus, pierced with a lance,
   have mercy on us.
Heart of Jesus, source of all consolation,
   have mercy on us.
Heart of Jesus, our life and resurrection,
   have mercy on us.
Heart of Jesus, our peace and our reconciliation,
   have mercy on us.
Heart of Jesus, victim for our sins,
   have mercy on us.
Heart of Jesus, salvation of those who trust in Thee,
   have mercy on us.
Heart of Jesus, hope of those who die in Thee,
   have mercy on us.
Heart of Jesus, delight of all the saints,
   have mercy on us.

Lamb of God, who takest away the sins of the world,
   spare us, O Lord.
Lamb of God, who takest away the sins of the world,
   graciously hear us, O Lord.
Lamb of God, who takest away the sins of the world,
   have mercy on us.

V. Jesus, meek and humble of heart.
R. *Make our hearts like to Thine.*

Let us pray: Almighty and eternal God, look upon the Heart of Thy most beloved Son and upon the praises and satisfaction which He offers Thee in the name of sinners; and to those who implore Thy mercy, in Thy great goodness, grant forgiveness in the name of the same Jesus Christ, Thy Son, who livest and reignest with Thee forever and ever. Amen.

Litany of the Blessed Virgin Mary

V. Lord, have mercy on us,

R. *Christ, have mercy on us.*

V. Lord, have mercy on us; Christ hear us,

R. *Christ, graciously hear us.*

God, the Father of heaven, *have mercy on us.*

God, the Son, Redeemer of the world, *have mercy on us.*

God, the Holy Spirit, *have mercy on us.*

Holy Trinity, one God, *have mercy on us.*

Holy Mary, *pray for us.*

Holy Mother of God, *pray for us.*

Holy Virgin of virgins, *pray for us.*

Mother of Christ, *pray for us.*

Mother of the Church, *pray for us.*

Mother of mercy, *pray for us.*

Mother of divine grace, *pray for us.*

Mother of hope, *pray for us.*

Mother most pure, *pray for us.*

Mother most chaste, *pray for us.*

Mother inviolate, *pray for us.*

Mother undefiled, *pray for us.*

Mother most amiable, *pray for us.*

Mother most admirable, *pray for us.*
Mother of good counsel, *pray for us.*
Mother of our Creator, *pray for us.*
Mother of our Savior, *pray for us.*
Virgin most prudent, *pray for us.*
Virgin most venerable, *pray for us.*
Virgin most renowned, *pray for us.*
Virgin most powerful, *pray for us.*
Virgin most merciful, *pray for us.*
Virgin most faithful, *pray for us.*
Mirror of justice, *pray for us.*
Seat of wisdom, *pray for us.*
Cause of our joy, *pray for us.*
Spiritual vessel, *pray for us.*
Vessel of honor, *pray for us.*
Singular vessel of devotion, *pray for us.*
Mystical rose, *pray for us.*
Tower of David, *pray for us.*
Tower of ivory, *pray for us.*
House of gold, *pray for us.*
Ark of the covenant, *pray for us.*
Gate of Heaven, *pray for us.*
Morning star, *pray for us.*
Health of the sick, *pray for us.*
Refuge of sinners, *pray for us.*
Solace of migrants, *pray for us.*
Comforter of the afflicted, *pray for us.*
Help of Christians, *pray for us.*
Queen of angels, *pray for us.*
Queen of patriarchs, *pray for us.*
Queen of prophets, *pray for us.*

Queen of Apostles, *pray for us.*
Queen of martyrs, *pray for us.*
Queen of confessors, *pray for us.*
Queen of virgins, *pray for us.*
Queen of all saints, *pray for us.*
Queen conceived without original sin, *pray for us.*
Queen assumed into Heaven, *pray for us.*
Queen of the Most Holy Rosary, *pray for us.*
Queen of families, *pray for us.*
Queen of peace, *pray for us.*

Lamb of God, who takest away the sins of the world,
   spare us, O Lord.
Lamb of God, who takest away the sins of the world,
   graciously hear us, O Lord.
Lamb of God, who takest away the sins of the world,
   have mercy on us.

V. Pray for us, O holy Mother of God.
R. *That we may be made worthy of the promises of Christ.*

Let us pray: Grant, O Lord God, we beseech Thee, that we Thy servants may rejoice in continual health of mind and body; and, through the glorious intercession of Blessed Mary ever Virgin, may be freed from present sorrow, and enjoy eternal happiness. Through Christ our Lord. Amen.

Litany of St. Joseph

Lord, have mercy on us. Christ, *have mercy on us.*
Lord, *have mercy on us.*
Christ, hear us. *Christ, graciously hear us.*

God the Father of Heaven, *have mercy on us.*
God the Son, Redeemer of the world, *have mercy on us.*
God the Holy Spirit, *have mercy on us.*
Holy Trinity, one God, *have mercy on us.*

Holy Mary, *pray for us.*
St. Joseph, *pray for us.*
Renowned offspring of David, *pray for us.*
Light of Patriarchs, *pray for us.*
Spouse of the Mother of God, *pray for us.*
Guardian of the Redeemer, *pray for us.*
Chaste guardian of the Virgin, *pray for us.*
Foster father of the Son of God, *pray for us.*
Diligent protector of Christ, *pray for us.*
Servant of Christ, *pray for us.*
Minister of salvation, *pray for us.*
Head of the Holy Family, *pray for us.*
Joseph most just, *pray for us.*
Joseph most chaste, *pray for us.*
Joseph most prudent, *pray for us.*
Joseph most strong, *pray for us.*
Joseph most obedient, *pray for us.*
Joseph most faithful, *pray for us.*
Mirror of patience, *pray for us.*
Lover of poverty, *pray for us.*
Model of artisans, *pray for us.*
Glory of home life, *pray for us.*
Guardian of virgins, *pray for us.*
Pillar of families, *pray for us.*
Support in difficulties, *pray for us.*
Solace of the wretched, *pray for us.*

Hope of the sick, *pray for us.*
Patron of exiles, *pray for us.*
Patron of the afflicted, *pray for us.*
Patron of the poor, *pray for us.*
Patron of the dying, *pray for us.*
Terror of demons, *pray for us.*
Protector of Holy Church, *pray for us.*

Lamb of God, who takest away the sins of the world,
   spare us, O Lord.
Lamb of God, who takest away the sins of the world,
   graciously hear us, O Lord.
Lamb of God, who takest away the sins of the world,
   have mercy on us.
V. He made him the lord of his household
R. And prince over all his possessions.

Let us pray: O God, in your ineffable providence you were pleased to choose Blessed Joseph to be the spouse of your most holy Mother; grant, we beg you, that we may be worthy to have him for our intercessor in heaven whom on earth we venerate as our Protector: You who live and reign forever and ever. Amen.

Selected Bibliography

Aquinas, St. Thomas. *The Summa Theologica*. Translated by the Fathers of the English Dominican Province. New York: Benziger Bros., 1947.

Augustine, St. *The Works of St. Augustine: A Translation for the 21st Century: Letters*. Edited by Boniface Ramsey. Translated by Roland J. Teske, S.J. Vol. 2. Hyde Park, NY: New City Press, 2003.

Benedict XVI, Pope. Post-synodal Apostolic Exhortation *Sacramentum Caritatis* (February 22, 2007).

——. Homily given at Saint Paul's Church in Luanda, Angola, March 21, 2009.

Benkovic, Johnnette. *Graceful Living: Meditations to Help You Grow Closer to God Day by Day*. Birmingham, AL: EWTN Publishing, 2016.

Book of Blessings. New York: Catholic Book Publishing, 1989.

Catechism of the Catholic Church, with *Glossary*, 2nd edition. Vatican City: Vatican Press, 1997.

Chervin, Ronda. *Quotable Saints*. Oak Lawn, IL: CMJ Marian Publishers, 2003.

The Code of Canon Law: in English Translation. London: Collins, 1983.

Compendium of the Catechism of the Catholic Church. Vatican City: Libreria Editrice Vaticana, 2005.

Congregation for Catholic Education. "Male and Female He Created Them": Towards a Path of Dialogue on the Question of Gender

Theory in Education. Vatican City: Congregation for Catholic Education, 2019.

Congregation for Divine Worship and the Discipline of the Sacraments. *Ordo Paenitentiae* (December 2, 1973).

———. Instruction *Redemptionis Sacramentum* (March 25, 2004).

Congregation for the Doctrine of the Faith. *Letter to the Bishops of the Catholic Church on Some Aspects of Christian Meditation* (October 15, 1989).

Congregation of Rites. Instruction *Eucharisticum Mysterium* (May 25, 1967).

The Didache, or Teaching of the Apostles. Edited and Translated by J. B. Lightfoot, 1885. Available at https://onlinechristianlibrary.com/wp-content/uploads/2019/05/didache.pdf.

Englebert, Omer. *The Lives of the Saints.* Translated by Christopher and Anne Fremantle. Lyndhurst, NJ: Barnes and Noble, 1994.

Escrivá, St. Josemaría. *Furrow.* Josemaría Escrivá. https://www.escrivaworks.org/book/furrow.htm.

———. *The Way.* Josemaría Escrivá, https://www.escrivaworks.org/book/the_way.htm.

Faber, Fr. Frederick. *The Blessed Sacrament: The Works and Ways of God.* London: Burns and Oates, 1861.

Francis, Pope. Bull of Indiction of the Extraordinary Jubilee of Mercy *Misericordiae Vultus.* (April 11, 2015).

———. *The Name of God Is Mercy.* Translated by Oonagh Stransky. New York: Random House, 2016.

Francis de Sales, St. *Introduction to the Devout Life.* Wheathampstead, Hertfordshire, England: Anthony Clark Books, 1962.

Ghezzi, Bert. *Voices of the Saints: A Year of Readings.* New York: Doubleday, 2000.

The Handbook of Indulgences: Norms and Grants. Totowa, NJ: Catholic Book Publishing, 1991.

Hardon, Fr. John A., S.J. *Modern Catholic Dictionary.* Kensington, MD: Inter Mirifica, 1999. Reprinted and published, Bardstown, KY: Eternal Life, 2nd printing, 2001.

Kowalska, St. Faustina. *Diary of St. Maria Faustina Kowalska, Divine Mercy in My Soul.* Stockbridge, MA: Marian Press, 1987.

John XXIII, Pope St. Encyclical *Paenitentiam Agere* (July 1, 1962).

John Paul II, Pope St. Address to the bishops of the Antilles on their Ad Limina visit, May 7, 2002.

———. Address to the bishops of the United States, Minor Seminary of Our Lady of the Angels (Los Angeles), September 16, 1987.

———. Address to the bishops of the United States on their Ad Limina visit, June 10, 1988.

———. Address to participants at a conference of the Apostolic Penitentiary, Rome, March 27, 2004.

———. Encyclical *Centesimus Annus* (May 1, 1991).

———. Post-synodal Apostolic Exhortation *Christifideles Laici* (December 30, 1988).

———. Encyclical *Dives in Misericordia* (November 30, 1980).

———. Letter *Dominicae Cenae* (February 24, 1980).

———. Encyclical *Ecclesia de Eucharistia* (April 17, 2003).

———. Encyclical *Evangelium Vitae* (March 25, 1995).

———. Encyclical *Fides et Ratio* (September 14, 1998).

———. Homily given at Aqueduct Racecourse, Brooklyn, New York, October 6, 1995.

———. Homily at Phoenix Park, Dublin, September 29, 1979.

———. Letter to Rev. George V. Coyne, S.J., June 1, 1988.

———. Apostolic Letter *Ordinatio Sacerdotalis* (May 22, 1994).

———. Post-synodal Apostolic Exhortation *Reconciliatio et Paenitentia* (December 2, 1984).

———. Post-synodal Apostolic Exhortation *Vita Consecrata* (March 25, 1996).

———. Wednesday Audience, January 16, 1980, on the Theology of the Body.

Lasance, Rev. F.X., and Rev. Francis Augustine Walsh, O.S.B. *The New Roman Missal.* New York: Benziger Brothers, 1942.

Lemoyne, Rev. Giovanni Battista, S.D.B. *The Biographical Memoirs of Saint John Bosco.* Translated by Rev. Diego Borgatello, S.D.B. New Rochelle: Salesiana Publishers, 1971.

Catholic Essentials

The Liturgy of the Hours. New York: Catholic Book Publishing, 1975.

Lucia, Fr. Martin, SS.CC. *Rosary Meditations from Mother Teresa of Calcutta: Loving Jesus with the Heart of Mary, Eucharistic Meditations on the Fifteen Mysteries of the Rosary*. N.p.: Missionaries of Charity, 1984.

Paone, Fr. Anthony J., S.J. *My Daily Bread*. Charlotte: TAN Books, 2015.

Paul VI, Pope St. Encyclical *Humanae Vitae* (July 25, 1968).

———. Message for the Day of Peace, January 1, 1972.

———. Encyclical Letter *Mysterium Fidei* (September 3, 1965).

———. Apostolic Letter *Solemni Hac Liturgia* (Credo of the People of God) (June 30, 1968).

Pius XII, Pope. Encyclical *Mystici Corporis Christi* (June 29, 1943).

"Quotes from Bishop Sheen." Archbishop Fulton John Sheen Spiritual Centre. http://www.archbishopfultonsheencentre.com/Quotes.html.

Schroeder, Fr. Frederick. *Every Day Is a Gift*. Totowa, NJ: Catholic Book Publishing, 1984.

Second Vatican Council. Decree on the Mission Activity of the Church *Ad Gentes* (December 2, 1965).

———. Decree on the Apostolate of the Laity *Apostolicam Actuositatem* (November 18, 1965).

———. Dogmatic Constitution on Divine Revelation *Dei Verbum* (November 18, 2965).

———. Pastoral Constitution on the Church in the Modern World *Gaudium et Spes* (December 7, 1965).

———. Declaration on Christian Education *Gravissimum Educationis* (October 28, 1965).

———. Dogmatic Constitution on the Church *Lumen Gentium* (November 21, 1964).

———. Decree on the Adaptation and Renewal of Religious Life *Perfectae Caritatis* (October 28, 1965).

———. Decree on the Ministry and Life of Priests *Presbyterorum Ordinis* (December 7, 1965).

———. Constitution on the Sacred Liturgy *Sacrosanctum Concilium* (December 4, 1963).

268

Teresa of Calcutta, Mother. *Love: A Fruit Always in Season, Daily Meditations from the Words of Mother Teresa of Calcutta.* Edited by Dorothy S. Hunt. San Francisco: Ignatius Press, 1987.

Teresa Benedicta of the Cross, St. *The Hidden Life: Essays, Meditations, Spiritual Texts.* Edited by L. Gelber and Michael Linssen, O.C.D. Translated by Waltraut Stein. Washington, D.C.: ICS Publications, 1992.

Thigpen, Paul. *A Dictionary of Quotes from the Saints.* Ann Arbor, MI: Servant Publications, 2001.

United States Conference of Catholic Bishops. *"Between Man and Woman": Questions and Answers About Marriage and Same-Sex Unions,* United States Conference of Catholic Bishops, https://www.usccb.org/topics/promotion-defense-marriage/between-man-and-woman-questions-and-answers-about-marriage-and.

———. *General Instruction of the Roman Missal.* Washington, D.C.: United States Conference of Catholic Bishops, 2010.

———. "Guidelines for the Reception of Communion" https://www.usccb.org/prayer-and-worship/the-mass/order-of-mass/liturgy-of-the-eucharist/guidelines-for-the-reception-of-communion.

———. *The Roman Missal,* English translation according to the Third Typical Edition. Totowa, NJ: Catholic Book Publishing, 2011.

Valiante, Francesco M. "On the Papacy of the Spiritual Director, Benedict XVI." EWTN. https://www.ewtn.com/catholicism/library/on-the-papacy-of-the-spiritual-director-benedict-xvi-1738.

"What Is the Theology of the Body?" Theologyofthebody.net.

About the Author

Fr. Wade L. J. Menezes, CPM, is a member of the Fathers of Mercy, a missionary preaching religious congregation based in Auburn, Kentucky. Ordained a priest during the Great Jubilee Year 2000, he received his bachelor of arts in Catholic thought from the Oratory of St. Philip Neri in Toronto, Canada, and his dual master of arts and master of divinity degrees in theology from Holy Apostles Seminary in Cromwell, Connecticut. His secular college degrees are in journalism and communications.

Fr. Wade has served as the Assistant General and as the Director of Vocations and Director of Seminarians for the Fathers of Mercy. He has also served as the chaplain in residence at the Shrine of the Most Blessed Sacrament of Our Lady of the Angels Monastery in Hanceville, Alabama (affiliated with Eternal Word Television Network). While at the shrine, Fr. Wade was a daily Mass celebrant, homilist, and confessor; he gave spiritual conferences on specialized points of Catholic Christian doctrine to the many pilgrims who visit the shrine. As an itinerant preacher for the Fathers of Mercy, he has preached throughout the United States, Canada, and Australia.

Fr. Wade has been a guest on various episodes of EWTN's *Mother Angelica Live* and *Life on the Rock*, during which he discussed such topics as the sanctification of marriage and family life, vocations, and the Sacred Liturgy. He has also hosted several televised series for EWTN, which have covered such topics as the necessity of the spiritual life, the Four Last Things, the Ten Commandments of Catholic Family Life, and the Gospel of Life versus the Culture of Death. He is host of the EWTN interstitial series *The Crux of the Matter*, *The Wonders of His Mercy*, and *In Defense of the Eucharist*. His many theological and doctrinal presentations have been featured on EWTN Global Catholic Radio, Ave Maria Radio, Guadalupe Radio Network, Covenant Network Radio, Catholic Broadcasting Northwest, and Voice of Virtue International. Fr. Wade is also the host of EWTN Global Catholic Radio's *Open Line Tuesday*.

Fr. Wade has been a contributing writer for the *National Catholic Register*, *Our Sunday Visitor*, *Catholic Twin Circle*, *Catholic Faith and Family*, the *Wanderer*, *Pastoral Life*, the *Catholic Faith*, *Lay Witness*, *Legatus*, and *Christian Ranchman*. Several homiletic series of his have appeared in *Homiletic and Pastoral Review*, an international journal for priests. Fr. Wade is the author of three books: *The Four Last Things: A Catechetical Guide to Death, Judgment, Heaven, and Hell*; *Overcoming the Evil Within: The Reality of Sin and the Transforming Power of God's Grace and Mercy*; and *Catholic Essentials: A Guide to Understanding Key Church Teachings* (from EWTN Publishing in conjunction with Sophia Institute Press).